CLOSET REDNECK

MAN THINGS I LEARNED IN THE OUTDOORS

RICK WATT A.D.D.

Copyright © 2014 by Rick Watt A.D.D.

Closet Redneck
Man Things I Learned In the Outdoors
by Rick Watt A.D.D.

Printed in the United States of America

ISBN 9781629522869

All rights reserved solely by the author. The author guarantees all contents are original and do not infringe upon the legal rights of any other person or work. No part of this book may be reproduced in any form without the permission of the author. The views expressed in this book are not necessarily those of the publisher.

Unless otherwise indicated, Bible quotations are taken from New International Version (NIV). Copyright © 1973, 1978, 1984, 2011 by Biblica, Inc.® Used by permission. All rights reserved worldwide.

www.xulonpress.com

MAN-LESSONS I LEARNED IN THE OUTDOORS

by Rick Watt, A.D.D. July .08

Welcome to my world! Let your wife know that you're going on a quick trip into this book, but the chapters are short and you'll be back in about 15 minutes. She won't mind. Come on in and explore the wonders of the outdoors from the comfort of your recliner. You will find that we have much in common. So, welcome to my mind. If you get lost in there, just fire three shots in the air, and I'll try to find you.

What is a Closet Redneck? Each time I put on the tie and jacket to do a wedding or funeral, in my heart I'm wearing camo. I grew up in the country, then in a small town, and back to the country again, but I have no confusion about the fact that I am not a city boy. I've walked through the downtown alleys and the deep woods hollows, and I love the hollows. Though I walk the narrow path, I notice every deer track crossing that path. Many people don't know this side of me... but the truth is I'm a redneck. Down deep in the heart of me is a guy who loves the woods, camping, cooking over a fire, and bringing down that big buck. NFL Football on a Sunday afternoon is better than any orchestra in the world. I'm a Closet Redneck.

I grew up in the woods of Pennsylvania. My hunting began at age 11 on a rabbit hunt with my Dad. We enjoyed the heavy snows and the sledding, with a huge fire at the bottom of the hill where we'd warm ourselves. My friends and I would play in the woods, run in the woods. We didn't need a cellphone, which was good because they weren't invented yet. We didn't stay home and watch TV or play video games. We were in the outdoors. We played army and hunting; we played in the cornfields and picked berries on the hillsides.

If you saw me in my everyday clothing, you might not know it. I don't wear a suit and tie, but I do wear blue jeans and a nice shirt. I reserve my camo for wearing at home and in the woods. I spend a lot of money at Gander Mountain, Bass Pro Shop, and from sportsmansguide.com to get my redneck clothes. I even have a really plush robe, but it is camo, so my wife can't find me when she has those "honey-do" jobs.

If you heard me speak in a church service, you'd never know that "this man is a redneck inside." But if you hunt with me or fish with me, you'll have no doubt. At one point in my life, I had three pickup trucks at once...and I was in my element.

If I had a choice of going to the movies or to the woods, the woods are where I'd be. If I had my choice of eating fine cuisine or slow-smoked barbecue, you'd find my homemade Bro's BBQ sauce dripping down my beard. Nobody knows that I sometimes get up every two or three hours during the night to feed the fire in the smoker in my backyard and keep that turkey, that pork roast, and those venison roasts smokin'.

As you read this book and my experiences, you'll find that in my private life, I am a redneck. My heart is in the woods, driving in the mud on a logging trail, soaked in scent blocker, and clothed in the redneck royal style – camouflage everything.

My friends and work associates may not know it, but they are looking at a woods-boy, a country-boy, a closet redneck. And you... you are reading the writing of one of your own.

INTRODUCTION: BEFORE WE START...

Guys, a lot of us are learning to be a husband, a dad, a fisherman, a hunter, a worker, or a golfer all at once. That's a lot of roles! We don't always feel confident, but we don't want to let anyone know we're not confident. **I'm here to remind you that other guys go through the same "junk" you deal with.** They have the same questions and doubts, they just don't tell anyone either. You're not alone, and you're probably not as unusual as you think.

If your friends seem to have it all together, they're pulling your leg, man! They're just like you and me. They have questions, doubts, aggravations, and fears. If you choose to hide your self-doubts, phobias, bad memories, or worries like the other guys, it's OK. I just don't want you to think you're the only one that has them. They fear snakes, bills, and their mother-in-law just like you do.

You'll find yourself smiling at the stuff I've written here because you've had some of the same ideas in your mind. We can learn from each other's adventures and mess-ups in life.

The stories in this book are true. Some names may be changed to protect the identity of the innocent, the guilty, and the ridiculously stupid. Anything "made-up" will be identified for you. Feel free to enjoy these stories or to use them around the campfire. Most hunters and fishermen don't need something to get us started telling our stories. Laugh at me if you want! I can take it. I enjoy my life, so you enjoy it, too.

When I say my stories are true, they are true to the best of my memory, as I remember them and as I felt them.

TABLE OF CONTENTS

Chapter One:	My First Hunting Trip	9
Chapter Two:	My First Deer	13
Chapter Three:	Duck Hunting and Laundromats	16
Chapter Four:	The Wonderful Filsons and Old Lady Wingard	18
Chapter Five:	My First Buck	21
Chapter Six:	The Alabama Guys and Scope Envy	24
Chapter Seven:	The Try, Try Again Buck	27
Chapter Eight:	We Boys and Our Cabins	29
Chapter Nine:	My Hunting Buddy, Dave	31
Chapter Ten:	Our First Adult Cabin	33
Chapter Eleven:	When the Rats Take Over	36
Chapter Twelve:	Bro's Barbecue Trailer	38
Chapter Thirteen:	Tackle Basketball	41
Chapter Fourteen:	The World's Worst Dolphin Fisherman...Me!	43
Chapter Fifteen:	Lost in Raccoon Land	47
Chapter Sixteen:	After the Coon Hunt– The Motorcyle Snow Storm	49
Chapter Seventeen:	Our New Cabin	52
Chapter Eighteen:	Another Misfire	55
Chapter Nineteen:	The No-Place-to-Hunt Georgia Buck	59
Chapter Twenty:	An Arrow Escape	62
Chapter Twenty-One:	Freezer Burned?	65
Chapter Twenty-Two:	An A.D.D. Hunter	67
Chapter Twenty-Three:	Would the Real Turkey Please Stand Up?	69
Chapter Twenty-Four:	The Legend of the Blind Buck	71
Chapter Twenty-Five:	My Best Buck so Far	74
Chapter Twenty Six:	The Best Bucks I've Ever Seen #1	77
Chapter Twenty-Seven:	The Best Buck I've Ever Seen #2	79
Chapter Twenty-Eight:	Taking the Long Shot	81
Chapter Twenty-Nine:	Dave, the Perfect Hunter	83
Chapter Thirty:	Mentoring an Expert	85
Chapter Thirty One:	My Second Son	87
Chapter Thirty-Two:	Hunting with My Younger Son	89

Chapter Thirty Three:	Mama's Boy (Don't You Mess with My Mama.)	91
Chapter Thirty-Four:	Scouting for a Life Partner—the Ultimate Hunt	93
Chapter Thirty-Five:	True Friends? When Friends Don't Want You Anymore	95
Chapter Thirty-Six:	Quicksand	98
Chapter Thirty-Seven:	The Darkest Fourth of July	100
Chapter Thirty-Eight:	Talkin' Turkey	102
Postlude:	Who am I?	105

CHAPTER ONE:
MY FIRST HUNTING TRIP

There I stood with my single-shot Savage .20 gauge shotgun and slug (we called 'em pumpkin balls). I really felt like a man, standing there with my gun, wearing my hunter clothes, license on my back! I was not afraid of the darkness and kept reminding myself of that as I stood there and heard the crunching sounds of some kind of animal pass by in the snow. "I'm not afraid of the darkness... I'm not afraid of the darkness." My creative mind began to imagine a bear, a bobcat, or the biggest buck in the state passing by safely in the darkness.

My earliest memory of hunting is Paul Wolf's rustic log cabin. The swayback-roofed structure sits along the Clarion River near Clarion, Pennsylvania. There was no electricity, so gas lights dimly lit the cabin. At night the light was yellowish and eerie, kind of otherworldly...like another dimension. This kind of thing is amazing to a kid. Sleep was deeper and food tasted better at the cabin. The group gathered around the wood stove and laughed loudly as they shared stories that may or may not have been true. Dad made me go to bed early because we'd get up before the sun, but I was too excited to sleep. I lay awake and listened, thrilled to be a part of this new experience of hunting. I was tucked under covers that were especially heavy, but so warm and comfortable. I lay there looking at the solid-log beams overhead and wondered if this was how pioneer kids felt as they lay in their beds at night.

The evening in the cabin was like a new world with the strange lighting and all the noise and laughter. Cabin life was too good to miss. Normal everyday things were an adventure. When someone had to go to the bathroom, everyone else laughed as that person put on their heavy clothes and boots and made the trip to the outhouse, about twenty yards away in the darkness through a shoveled path in the deep snow that kept filling in with the new snow. The "outhouse flashlight" hung on a hook for everyone to use. I thought about this outhouse thing, a hole in the ground with a little building over it and wondered about the floor and how old it was. What if the rotten floor gave way and I was dropped into the pit below? What a way to die... sinking slowly into the...that was my last thought as I dropped off to sleep. I don't remember dreaming about outhouses...and that's a good thing.

I awakened to the smell of bacon and eggs frying. Every bite tasted so good. The gas lights in the morning darkness made the food look as good as it tasted. Dad said it was long-john time, so I bundled up, but couldn't bend over at all, with all of those layers of clothes, to tie my boots. Dad tied them for me. I can still see him there kneeling and tightening. Those were Woolrich days and my colors were red and black plaid, before the days of hunter orange. My Pennsylvania hunting license hung from my back, displayed for all the world to see... hunter-cool, but warm in my wool.

I had heard the door open and close many times during the night, but now I discovered that those folks never made it to the outhouse. With the flashlight I saw a ring of yellow in the snow, about a foot out, that completely surrounded the porch. I decided to add to the ring, and with great difficulty wrestled the Woolrich pants zipper, the long underwear, and my regular underwear out of the way, careful not to let anything get on my clothes. My circle didn't quite reach the others at that time of my life, but I made my mark in the snow.

The woods were black as we entered. The men would not use a flashlight. They knew the path. I tried to stay close to Dad, but I ran face-first into several trees. We climbed and climbed the mountain, and it seemed that the uphill grade never stopped. Since my legs were shorter, I took two steps to their one, thankful that it would be all downhill on the return trip at the end of the day. I was young and healthy, but my heart was pumping wildly from the excitement and effort.

When we arrived at my place to stand, Dad stomped down the snow at the foot of a tree and told me to stand there and try not to budge. The stomping, he said, was so that I would not make crunching sounds if I moved. He showed me the direction where he would be standing and let me know that when the sun came up, I'd be able to see him. "Don't shoot in that direction," he said, "and only bucks with antlers."

When the sun came up, I began to count the deer that passed. I was up to none-in-a-row when Dad motioned me to come to him. Paul Wolf had joined him and they were pulling out sandwiches. There's only one thing better than food in the woods, and that is the relief of peeing in the woods, which I had to do. Dad gave that impatient look, and they began to look around for a good place to send me. Then the eyes of both men seemed to drift to the same direction at once and Paul whispered, "Bust him, Dick." Dad raised the .270 Remington that I use today and the gun cracked. "He's down," yelled Paul. I tried to figure out why we whispered before and we were yelling now. The two men were now slow in the woods, but I wasn't. I raced in the direction he had shot to see the deer that I hadn't seen. Suddenly, there he was, six points on his antlers. He was struggling to stand and I easily overtook him. Suddenly I didn't know what to do. He stopped and just looked at me. Paul and Dad arrived and said, "Finish him, Rick," which I did immediately. I forgot all about having to pee.

It was downhill all the way and the deer slid easily across the top of the deep snow as we dragged him back to the cabin. They hung the six-pointer up where passers-by in their cars could see it and be envious...then went inside. I wasn't cold after helping to drag the deer, and I stayed outside and stared.

There was also the possibility that those driving by might think it was my deer. Another hunter with us nailed a spike buck and hung him alongside. I stood by the six-pointer so they wouldn't think the spike was mine. That's where my memory ends, except that everyone ate deer liver for supper and once I tasted it, I determined that all my deer livers in the future would be given to others. I'm just not a liver kind of guy.

My parents divorced, so I didn't have a lot of experiences with my Dad, but I will always remember this one and smile. Dad is gone now and I am 57 years old as I write. My sons, Chris and Philip, are young men now. I just hope I have given them memories like this one to share with their kids.

INSIGHT ONE: Dads, when you take your son (or daughter) hunting you are making memories and creating an adventure for your boy (or girl). For your child, it is an adventure. Be patient if he doesn't "get it." When he messes up, just laugh together and share with him/her about the mistakes you made as a boy. Share some of the adventures of your own childhood. For those first few years, dedicate the season to your son or daughter. Your child is your trophy right now. I don't have that many memories of my dad when I was a child, because my folks divorced and he moved out. If you're a very busy dad or a dad who only sees his kids on weekends, make those times memorable, Dad. Let your children have memories that make them smile. If you're a Dad who lives with his children, make a lot of memories.

Several years ago my son revealed to me that he doesn't really like deer-hunting that much. The boy has never missed a deer and has shot quite a number of them. He continued, "I just go to spend the time with you, Dad." I was touched and disappointed at the same time. I knew our hunting days were coming to an end, and I also knew that my son loved his dad...and that was a great moment in my life.

INSIGHT TWO: Make each journey a part of the adventure. Hunting with your child has less to do with downing a big buck than it does with bonding with the son or daughter God gave you. He or she is going to go through changes and stages where you will be regarded as not-having-a-clue. In those teen years, this same child will likely wonder when you got so stupid. The moments you spend in the woods fishing, hunting, or just in the yard throwing the football have little to do with fishing, hunting, or football. They are about connection. They will help both of you through those adolescent years. The time and experience that you share is more valuable than some trophy on the wall.

Dads, here's something to tell your son when he strikes out at the ball game, when he misses the big buck or sneezes and scares the big'un away. Just look him eye to eye and say, **"You know, these times are more about you and me being together, son, than about homeruns and big bucks."**

At least in my case, the "gang" of friends hanging out in the cabin, the food we cooked over the fire, the friendly jabs of jokes about each other, the stories (exaggerations?) that were shared about the big ones that got away really made hunting an experience of relationships. I will treasure those friendships all my life. Truth is, if I had the chance to go to a tremendous area with a bunch of guys and had to be the cook for the whole trip, I'd go for it. Guys, it isn't just about getting a buck! *(Side note, with all humility: but I usually do!)*

INSIGHT THREE: If I had to say, "I am not afraid", I must have been a little bit afraid on that dark morning under that tree. Otherwise, I wouldn't have brought it up. Fear is not the same as cowardice. A brave man is not necessarily the man who goes forward with no fear. He is often the man who goes forward in spite of fear. **When the thing we are aiming toward becomes more important than the thing we are afraid of, we begin to conquer our fears.**

If an eight-hundred-pound grizzly is charging and your gun jams and you are not afraid, you are what we call DUMB. If you gather your senses and simply outrun your hunting buddy, then he gets the chance to be fearless.

Sometimes we let our kids think we aren't afraid of anything, so they feel very inferior, like there's something wrong with them for being afraid. Maybe we ought to be honest with ourselves and with them and explain how that we get afraid, but we can't let fear stop us from doing what we should do, and that those little and big fears will always "pop up" in life. Overcoming fear is a normal part of life.

2 Timothy 1:7: For God did not give us a spirit of timidity (fear),

but a spirit of power, of love and of self-discipline.

CHAPTER TWO:
MY FIRST DEER

Putting an end to my father's downed buck was not so fulfilling as bagging my first deer on my own. It happened in the snow in McKean County in northwestern Pennsylvania.

It was doe season, and we spent the night in the back of our station wagon in the freezing cold with sleeping bags. There was my step Dad, my step brother, and myself in the back of the wagon with the seats laid flat. It was cold, uncomfortable and crowded. I soon became unconscious of the gas being passed by the two others...and the snoring. The gas could have had me unconscious on its own, but somehow avoiding freezing to death was more important, and I didn't mind their large, stinky, noisy presence (much) because they were warm. I wondered if my future wife would feel that way about me on cold winter nights. (She does!)

Breakfast tasted great as the eggs were cooked in a black pan over an open fire outside. We had used a snow shovel to clear a big circle where the fire was built. Bill (my step Dad) just fried the bacon first, and then threw the eggs in that bacon grease. This is very unhealthy but wonderfully tasty on a snowy morning. We even made our own toast on three-pronged sticks over the fire.

Bill Stokes joined us with his jeep and we drove up the logging trail in about two feet of snow. Mr. Stokes had two front seats, but the back was a place where you sat on the metal wheel well and held on for dear life (deer life?). At the top of the mountain, we jumped out of the jeep and our feet sunk deeply into the snow. Bill (step dad) took his own son, and Bill Stokes said, "You come with me, Rick." On his hip was a Colt .45 stainless steel revolver with a scope. This was his doe gun. I carried a .32 special lever-action Winchester Model 94 rifle. The shells ejected out the top and though one could get a side-mount scope, I didn't own one. It didn't matter. I was confident and doing well at targets set at 100 yards with the peep sights.

Well, we lifted our feet up, set 'em down, then lifted them again through that high snow. There was that crunching sound of the compacted snow as your foot finally made it through to the ground. The progress was terrible, but the visibility was great. Before long we could see deer moving in the distance between the trees. These were big woods with big trees. The deer were there and then gone, there and then gone. Bill took me by the shoulders and whispered, "there are a couple broadside...they'll be the easiest."

Now, I'm not the guy to always take the easy way and I could see that the biggest deer was facing us between two trees with only a chest shot. From behind, Bill put his hands on my shoulders and breathed, "Just take aim and squeeze that trigger." I know I sound like this all took a long time, but it didn't. I lined up on the chest of the big doe facing us and squeezed the trigger. Funny thing is I didn't see the deer go down, but Bill did. He was whooping and hollering, "You should have seen her stand up on her hind legs and flop over," he yelled. This guy made me feel the excitement of the moment, and I felt like a man and like I had a friend who celebrated my victory with me. We made our way over to where she was, a big girl and my first deer. Now it was my turn to whoop and holler. So I whooped and hollered!

We got a four-foot piece of pine branch and tied the rope to it so that both of us could pull her along. She skimmed along the top of the snow like a toboggan, but we still were stepping way up and sinking way down. Even in the cold, we both broke a sweat. When we got to the jeep, Bill Stokes bragged about my shot. My step dad just smiled a little to the other Bill and changed the subject. No response to me. Later, I got to see that Colt .45 pistol in action. It was amazing as he drew it smoothly, brought it up, squeezed it off, and the running deer went down. Y'know, that man was good to me that day. I wasn't used to that, but it sure was nice when it happened.

INSIGHT ONE: Guys, notice your kids...step kids, too! You're the adult. Be the main encourager in their lives. If they resist you, be the adult and love them. Even when they are rebelling, correct them, but give your approval when you can. They need it, even if they don't know they need it. There is no statement made in my life with more impact than when my real father, after a church service where I had preached, said, "You are really good."

INSIGHT TWO: Why shoot the biggest deer when it is a harder target to shoot? Why not go for the easier, smaller, broadside deer? **The easy way isn't always the best way.** The things we attain through the greatest effort are the greatest rewards in themselves. **When a man works hard to succeed, he enjoys his success more.**

INSIGHT THREE: You aren't going to get approval or encouragement from everyone for the things you accomplish. (Read that again, friend.) Some folks never say anything positive to anyone, and others may just not like you. It's OK! If not everyone liked Jesus, why would you think they'd all like you? Live with it! Everyone else has to live with the same realization. **You're normal if not everyone likes you.**

INSIGHT FOUR: If you require the approval and backing of people, you will not accomplish much in your life. Even without the applause of others, there is a great satisfaction in overcoming hurdles, working hard, and succeeding. Approval, support, and cheers are nice fringe benefits, but not requirements on the way to success. Go for it, man!

> **Sometimes the adventure of trying, or the final results of our efforts, are encouragement enough.** There may be some folks who will criticize how you did it or how much time it took you to do it. Those who say such things are usually the ones who never accomplish anything. **Every person who ever did something great had others who laughed or scoffed at him.** There's Noah, whose neighbors must have laughed and mocked like crazy. Look at Christopher Columbus and those who were sure that this lunatic would die by sailing off the edge of the flat earth. Look at "Seward's Folly," as cohorts and newsmen ridiculed our acquisition of Alaska as a part of the U.S.A. I wonder how much oil we've gleaned from that purchase? Look at those who mocked Jesus on the cross. They felt sure that he had failed. He didn't. Even if the majority mocks you, that majority can be wrong. Why do you need the approval of those who accomplish nothing?

Matthew 5:11: Blessed are you when people insult you, persecute you and falsely say all kinds of evil against you because of me.
12 Rejoice and be glad, because great is your reward in heaven, for in the same way they persecuted the prophets who were before you.

CHAPTER THREE:
DUCK HUNTING AND LAUNDROMATS

I've only been duck hunting twice in my life. I'd like to try it again, but no one who knows me will take me. It's like I have a DO-NOT-TAKE-DUCK-HUNTING sign on my back. Those swamps have a way of pulling me in...literally, and both of my hunts ended with my hip waders filled with water.

You see, my Dad and I went after the elusive duck when I was very young. I wore my hip waders from trout fishing. Dad drove to this marshy place where we would meet other hunters who had a duck blind out on the water. Note that I said "out on the water." It took 30 yards of wading to get to the blind. Dad took all our stuff, and I took care of myself and my .20 gauge while wearing those hip waders. About midway to the blind, I got stuck in the mud and began to lean this way and that way to get out. You guessed it! I lost my balance and ended up sitting down in the water. It would have been up to my knees if I'd been standing up (plus several inches of mud). I wasn't standing up, though, and in my sitting position, the water was up to my chest and running down the inside of those waders to my freezing cold toes. In the meantime, I held the .20 gauge high in the air with one arm.

Dad got that "this is incredible" look on his face as time froze... along with my butt and toes. Then he pretty much carried me, my .20 gauge, and his .12 gauge the rest of the way to the blind, where I was instructed to take off my waders, my shoes, socks, shirt, pants, and pretty much everything except my long-johns. It was very cold and windy.

The adults got a lot of ducks, but I never picked up my gun. I just sat there soaked, on a bench, shivering. I wondered why I hadn't stayed in bed. My other clothes hung on various nails in the blind and were becoming frozen stiff. That should give you a clue as to what was happening to the long-johns and my body. About noon Dad had me put the waders back on as he carried my shoes, my socks, my shirt and pants, my coat, my .20 gauge, his .12 gauge, and helped me to shore. We went to the car and drove to town to a laundromat where I sat in the car with the heater while Dad dried all my clothes. When people walked by, I just sunk lower and lower in the seat. The car heater was actually helping dry the long-johns.

Dad came out and tossed the clothes to me. "Are we going out hunting again?" I asked. I can't describe the look on Dad's face...but I could tell that the answer was "no." My question wasn't really out of my enthusiasm to wade again, but out of a desire not to ruin his duck hunting day.

Dad was persistent, however. About two years later we tried it again, and again I was in the blind in my wet long johns. Why break a tradition? This time I still shot at the ducks. Didn't get one, as I shook with cold, but shot at 'em. Oh yes, during our two-time legacy of duck hunting, we included the laundromat in both excursions. Maybe someday I'll find a retriever who is big enough to bring ME back to the blind from the water.

INSIGHT ONE: Some of the funniest things that ever happen to us were not funny at that moment. Just when you're ready to celebrate and have fun, you're stuck in the mud, you've got a flat tire, you're embarrassed in front of friends. There's nothing funny about that, right? Later, however, we may find ourselves chuckling on those memories. They can become our favorite stories to share among friends. Are things rough right now? Keep going. Life is too short to dwell on the times you're stuck in your wet long-johns with chuckling hunters and a disappointed Dad.

Did I ever become a better duck hunter? Hey, I was a fine duck hunter, just a lousy wader.

INSIGHT TWO: Sometimes we need to focus not on our disappointment, but on being thankful for the remedies. Thank goodness for laundromats. This situation really was embarrassing, humiliating, and physically painful. I'm just so glad that someone built a laundromat in that town. My dry clothes were so warm and felt so good.

Matthew 6:34: Therefore do not worry about tomorrow, for tomorrow will worry about itself.
Each day has enough trouble of its own.

CHAPTER FOUR:
THE WONDERFUL FILSONS AND OLD LADY WINGARD

In another memory-corner of my younger life are Mr. and Mrs. Filson. I hope you had someone like them. They were the oldest people I knew, and they owned a really nice home on about 10 acres of land on the other side of my friend Jimmy Gordon's house. They had hedges that made their property like another world to enter, and they welcomed us. We would join them in their back yard, and she would go in and bring out iced tea or popsicles for everyone. It was like knowing Mr. and Mrs. Santa Claus, year-round.

Mr. Filson would often work on the various plants and flowers in that huge yard, and I thought it was fun to go and work with him. *(Funny how work wasn't as much fun at my own house.)* They were like having grandparents right in the midst of the neighborhood. We were all great friends.

Another neighbor was Old Lady Wingard. I didn't create that name. She stayed to herself and yelled at the kids who trespassed on her front yard. Some of the kids said she was a witch, and some were really afraid of her. At Halloween the kids threw loose corn at her windows to taunt her and ran when she came outside.

I could never get out of my mind that Mrs. Wingard had no friends, so one day I went to her door. Her eyes flashed with anger as she answered the doorbell. Most kids who rang her doorbell did so and ran. "My name is Rick and I'm your neighbor," I said, "and I've come to visit." Her next expression was shock, then softening. I wasn't the most cultured kid, so I sat down on her porch and just expected her to do the same. She could have been offended by my boldness, but she wasn't. She said, "Just a minute." Was she getting her magic wand to turn me into a toad? Nope, she got two glasses of ice water and came and sat on the step with me. I didn't know anything about being "careful" about what I said. I asked her if she'd ever been married or had kids? She hadn't. Had she always lived in our town? I guess God gave me wisdom to concentrate on being interested in her. We finished quickly and she said she needed to go in now, but she added, "You can come back again, Rick." I did!

Several years ago, Mrs. Wingard died, and to my surprise left me her property and possessions, valued at about $450,000. Gotcha! She didn't really leave me anything, but I was the only one in the world allowed to hunt in the 40 acres of pine trees behind her house until she died. That is not what I wanted. I just wanted to be a friend to someone who didn't have any friends...and I was. I was Mrs. Wingard's friend.

INSIGHT ONE: There are a few people who maintain that childlike joy through their adult life and many of them drive us nuts. Here they come with their Pollyana attitudes, finding the best in everything and everyone. I try to be one of those. I don't always succeed.

On the other hand are the normal cynics who always complain and find fault with everything and everyone. Their kids, their parents, the teachers at school, the pastor at church, the neighbor next door...everyone falls short of their expectation, including themselves. The positive ones are stupidly happy while we are intelligently miserable, right? Read that one again. (Stupidly happy? Intelligently miserable?) Who is right? Which one is really smart?

What a difference it can be to decide to be happy before tomorrow comes. What if you and I decided to be a party looking for a place to happen, rather than a critic ready to find fault? When we remember to look for the good stuff and thank God for it, we realize all the good things we might have missed by being critical, and we please God because He loves our praise. He gave you the good stuff to enjoy.

Being nice shocks people! I like to do that. Have you ever realized how much power you have to totally change someone's day? Just when no one's expecting it, you tell your wife or your mom what an incredible meal that was and how fortunate you are to have someone that's such a great cook. Give 'em a hug or kiss and then go watch the football game. Leave them in shock!

INSIGHT TWO: There are miserably lonely people out there who proclaim, "I don't need anyone." They believe it, but they are wrong. **God made us to need others. He made others to need us!** Oh, I can hear some of you saying, "No one wants me. I don't even want me." That's the problem with folks who are negative. When it's YOU, no matter where you go, there YOU are. The only escape is death or change. Death doesn't sound too good. How do we change?

Find someone miserable and unlikeable and find something good to say to them about themselves. Yes, they'll be suspicious, but withdraw quickly so that you can come the next time with something else good. Soon they'll look forward to the only source of encouragement in their life where they had none before...YOU! Ask for nothing, but give encouragement. Don't be sickening, but be seriously positive. Leave them wanting more, rather than wishing the encounter was over. Wouldn't it be great if some folks just "lit up" when you enter the room because they know something good is coming?

> *Matthew 25:33: He will put the sheep on his right and the goats on his left. 34 "Then the King will say to those on his right, 'Come, you who are blessed by my Father; take your inheritance, the kingdom prepared for you since the creation of the world. 35 For I was hungry and you gave me something to eat, I was thirsty and you gave me something to drink, I was a stranger and you invited me in, 36 I needed clothes and you clothed me, I was sick and you looked after me, I was in prison and you came to visit me.' 37 "Then the righteous will answer him, 'Lord, when did we see you hungry and feed you, or thirsty and give you something to drink? 38 When did we see you a stranger and invite you in, or needing clothes and clothe you? 39 When did we see you sick or in prison and go to visit you?' 40 "The King will reply, 'I tell you the truth, whatever you did for one of the least of these brothers of mine, you did for me.'*

CHAPTER FIVE:
MY FIRST BUCK

The snow had been light, and the leaves were "crunchy" underfoot as we walked the gas-line to our deer stands. Suddenly the woods became alive as what seemed like 20 deer ran by us unseen in the darkness, their hooves crunching on the icy leaves. My heart pounded and my mind asked, "Does this mean the deer have run off to other places and won't be where we're hunting?" Hey, I was a kid, but I'd already learned not to ask dumb questions aloud, or risk facing ridicule and laughter. I'd ask someone else later.

The light began to break, and I had a beautiful view of the opening through the woods. I was standing on the ground at the base of a tree on the natural gas pipeline, where I had carefully scraped away all debris that could make a sound if I shifted. You may remember that my Dad taught me that on our first hunting trip. The next sound I heard was a loud CRACK from the top of the hill, and down through the trees trotted a 3-point buck. He never stopped, but I raised and fired before he disappeared over the next bench of the hillside. I wanted to pursue right away, but I waited, as I didn't know these woods, and we weren't to move from our stand for fear of coming into the sightline of another hunter. I figured the deer had dropped just out of sight. It had been a good shot, and I was certain I had hit him well.

My older step brother came along, and we quietly sneaked to the edge to overlook below, where a good blood trail showed the direction of the deer. Suddenly the deer struggled to stand just 20 yards away, and as I raised my .32 Special, my step brother fired his 30.06 and dropped him. There was no challenge to the shot, but he took it and he claimed the deer. Besides the blood trail, the deer was spewing pieces of lung, and the place where he had been laying was full of blood. When we had dragged the deer up the hill (that's the problem with chasing them downhill) my Step Dad approached, and I listened as my step brother told how that I had barely wounded the deer on the shoulder, and he had to shoot it to keep it from getting away. I started to speak, "That deer was hit in the—" but Bill cut me off with his comment, "Just in the shoulder...it's Dick's deer." That was the end of the conversation, because the king had spoken and I could only expect the two to make jokes about it if I said anything more. They whispered and chuckled anyway.

What they had to say did not change the truth. I needed to be secure in myself enough to know the truth and feel good. Unfortunately, at that time I wasn't secure in myself, and I spent many days and nights wishing things were different. I questioned my value as a kid. Why did my step Dad and step brother always put me down? I wondered how many kids felt like I did. This helped teach me to be more aware of other people, though. I would go out and build people, not tear them down, and after a lot of healing, I am doing that today. Are you healing from anything tough?

INSIGHT ONE: People are sometimes going to take credit for what you have done. It's tough, but you need to decide whether it is important enough to fight the battle or if this is one you just can't win and doesn't matter. Most of the things we do aren't for "credit" anyway, but doesn't it stink when the louse who does nothing steals the credit? Remember that his boss will expect him to do it again...and he can't. You can just know in your heart that you did a good job, no matter who got the credit. Revenge is an empty triumph.

INSIGHT TWO: There are going to be conflicts in life, but you get to choose which battlefields you are willing to die on. I used to fight every battle. Another battle would begin before the first one was resolved. Life became a constant battle and even when I won, I couldn't enjoy it. This is true in marriage, family life, at work, and everywhere you live. So I'm still learning to choose my battlefields and avoid a lot of conflicts that really don't matter, while taking a stand when it's worthwhile.

INSIGHT THREE: Bullies come in all shapes and sizes. Some use physical abuse, while others attack the emotional, relational, and mental health. In high school, it may be the elite kids who look down on everyone who is not in their group. You may have a boss who's a bully or some co-worker who takes delight in overpowering others and putting them down in front of others. It can be a spouse, man or woman who just tends to control and dominate. Just remember that the guy or gal has a problem which led to their need to dominate. If you don't have that need, then you're healthy. Don't let his or her problem become yours. **I just don't like bullies. I never want to BE one.**

2 Corinthians 13:5: Examine yourselves to see whether you are in the faith;
test yourselves. Do you not realize that Christ Jesus is in you—unless, of course, you fail the test?
Ephesians 6:4: Fathers, do not exasperate your children. Instead bring them up
in the nurture (feed their needs) and admonition (gentle correction) of the Lord.

CHAPTER SIX:
THE ALABAMA GUYS AND SCOPE ENVY

We'd just moved to Alabama, and this was a new hunting place with a different bunch of guys. There was only one guy I knew, the one who brought me to this club. I was a husband now, and not so concerned with what others thought; and it's a good thing. All the "good ol' boys pulled out their powerful scopes on expensive rifles, and I pulled out my .32 special Winchester, Model 94 lever action rifle like the cowboys used (maybe the cowboys were 30-30s) with iron sights.

One of the not-so-kind and sensitive hunters laughed and asked, "Are you gonna use THAT?" Another replied, "this is scope country, boy" (the word "boy" has two syllables in Alabama...but I can't spell it). You won't be shooting under 100 yards." I looked at the thick woods we were going to hunt and knew my stand was in the woods, not on the fields. "Let's see what those scopes can do," I replied stupidly. Out came the sandbags and spotting scopes onto the hood of the jeep. They were shooting silver-dollar sized (the old-sized silver dollar) groupings in the bullseye from anchored and padded rests on the hoods of the jeep. Why had I opened my big mouth? "Tell you what guys," I said, "I'll be shooting offhand in the woods unless I find a good rest in the right place. Do you see the place where your cardboard target was folded across and up and down? It made a plus sign there." They all shook their heads, grinning at each other. *(If you'd asked me what I was doing, I'd have had to say, "I have no idea" but I went on.)* "I'm going to drill that intersection where the two lines come together." I raised up, offhand, pulled back the hammer and fired...scope-less. God is soooo good, guys. I drilled that intersection of the folds, slid my gun into its case and said, "I think I'll be OK."

I couldn't have made that shot again in a million years. It was my gun and I often hit the bullseye, but never had it felt so good. I didn't get a shot at a deer that day, and that was OK. I had gained acceptance into the group of "good ol' boys" and nothing was ever said about their scopes again. *(Meanwhile, I began to shop for a .270 with a scope.)*

INSIGHT ONE: Men enjoy a little head-buttin' with each other. Little boys pick fights. We big boys are more sophisticated about it. I really enjoy the jousting sometimes and the good-natured jabs with my friends.

As I get older, it becomes easier to do the thing of esteeming someone else to make him look good. It's said that the 2nd dog in the sled team always has the same view. You can figure that one out, but there is only one lead dog per team. Besides the 2nd dog, there's a 3rd, and a 4th, and a 5th, and on. Sometimes and in some places we get to be the lead dog, while in others we show our real strength in being willing to be a part of the team without the primary glory and position. Sometimes I'm glad not to be the lead-guy, because I don't have to carry all the responsibility. Truth is, though, I occasionally still enjoy a little good-natured head-buttin' with the other guys.

When I'm at the office, my secretary makes me look better than I am, and she takes joy in doing so. All of you supervisors know what I mean. Can't play quarterback? Get a great one and be happy that the team is winning. **Competition makes our free enterprise system great, but the truth is that cooperation makes our country great, our company great, our friendships great, and our family great.**

INSIGHT TWO: Don't be bluffed by your own bluff. God doesn't want us to hate ourselves, but neither does He want us to be deceived that we are the "best." **If you are the best now...look out, you'll get older, slower, retire, and die.** Younger guys will smile, knowing they can now beat you. Whether you are Mohammed Ali, Billy Graham, Babe Ruth, Peyton Manning, or whomever...you can't stay the best. **Just be YOUR best.**

So what do we do? We DO our best and sometimes we excel. Other times we blow it. Look up how many times Babe Ruth struck out, how many times Thomas Edison failed as he experimented, how many shots Michael Jordan missed. You will go through tough times and great ones. Learn from the tough ones and learn from (and enjoy) the great ones, too. **Only God is perfect. Strive for it, but know you will seldom if ever hit it.**

INSIGHT THREE: The majority can be wrong! The ridicule of the good ol' boys didn't change the fact that my .32 special Model 94 Winchester was a fine gun. It served me through a lot of years and brought down a bunch of deer. I was comfortable and familiar with what it could and couldn't do, and I was pretty good with it. **Don't let any opinion of others affect the truth that you know.** Theirs is an unknowing opinion. Yours is a truth learned through experience. Smile at their laughter and secretly know that they have no idea what they are talking about. Make 'em wonder what you've got. It's OK that your values are different than theirs! Appreciate what you've got and be happy.

Matthew 15:20: And when they had mocked him, they took off the purple robe
and put his own clothes on him. Then they led him out to crucify him.
(Jesus knew exactly who He was!)

CHAPTER SEVEN:
THE TRY, TRY AGAIN BUCK

In the early morning, I had climbed into an apple tree. There was a simple ladder and a small platform between the first split of branches. The surrounding branches gave enough cover, so I didn't need further camouflage. I knew this was a good place to be, as I'd been here and taken deer before. There he was, a small six point moving out of the woods about 60 yards away. It was buck season and time for some venison in the freezer. By this time I had moved on to a .270 Ruger M77 Lightweight Rifle with a nice 6-9x Redfield wide-view scope.

What a beautiful shot this would be. I raised the gun smoothly for the broadside shot. I squeezed the trigger softly and "click." That's right…"click." I'd heard of guys dumb enough to forget to put a shell in the chamber, but I didn't think I was one of them. I quietly bolted back smoothly and there was the shell in there. I checked for the firing pin imprint and there it was. Bad shells? I tried to be quiet as I inserted another shell into the chamber and looked up. My hands were steady, and I was confident.

The buck had moved…closer to me…only 40 yards now, and he conveniently turned broadside. I was so ready. Squeeze and "click." Unbolting was not as quiet this time as I had begun to shake like a first-time hunter seeing his first buck. This little buck was becoming very important to me. The bolt rattled and the new shell did, too, as I tried to hit-the-hole. When chambered, I looked up and the buck was 20 feet away. He still had not winded or seen me. I raised the gun and squeezed…a sure thing…"click." The buck now turned to walk into the woods. I had a quartering shot and bolted the new shell in quickly. I didn't care about noise. He stopped and turned at the edge of the woods when he heard the noise of my bolt…BOOM! The buck was down. I was soaked with sweat and it wasn't hot. I was shaking and this was not a big buck. I was excited, because though I didn't know what was wrong with the gun, I had finally succeeded.

INSIGHT ONE: Little challenges can become very big ones when the difficulty level is raised. That buck became precious when it looked like he would get away. How great it would be if we looked at every tough challenge of life that way and enjoyed every victory to the maximum.

INSIGHT TWO: Things go wrong. Sometimes they are our own fault, and sometimes they are someone else's. In fact, **sometimes there is no fault to be found, just an obstacle to be overcome.** I found out that my firing pin was hardly long enough to set off the shells; and the gunsmith took care of that really quickly. Getting mad in the tree wouldn't have helped. Becoming frustrated and wondering which of my buddies messed with my gun as a big joke would have led to wrong thinking. I just kept trying, and trying, and trying until BOOM...success. It wasn't until AFTER the crisis that I was able to seek and remedy the cause.

INSIGHT THREE: When you have a crisis in life, sometimes you need to deal with the feelings and problems at hand before you can seek the cause and solve the problem. That is often the case in relating with other people. I prefer to deal with the facts first. Others often don't care about the facts, just about how they feel. Deal with their feeling first. Be patient, not frustrated, and don't give up. Sometimes when their feelings are dealt with, the facts look pretty small and manageable.

INSIGHT FOUR: If at first you don't succeed...decide whether to try again or decide to pursue a different objective. Why do some of us try to make something work that has never worked? Trying to get rich quick? Don't starve in the meantime. Find a job that brings in cash to feed the family and pay the mortgage while you pursue your dream. I know musicians and inventors that spent their whole life passing up incredible jobs because they were going to make it big. Some do, but none of my friends did. Keep trying if it's a worthwhile goal, but make certain that other areas of your life are taken care of. Consider that sometimes our way just doesn't work, and we need to try new methods and direction.

Luke 9:23: Then he said to them all: "If anyone would come after me, he must deny himself and take up his cross daily and follow me.
24 For whoever wants to save his life will lose it, but whoever loses his life for me will save it.
25 What good is it for a man to gain the whole world and yet lose or forfeit his very self?"

CHAPTER EIGHT:
WE BOYS AND OUR CABINS

I grew up in the country. Across Highway 422 from our house was the farm of Beryl and Mary Fuller. My two younger brothers and I had so much fun on their farm. I'll always remember picking wild grapes (with permission) and carrying home multiple shopping bags and buckets so that mom could make homemade grape jelly. Somehow it tasted better when you picked the grapes yourself and smelled the scent of Mom cooking them on the stove before they were transformed into jelly.

This was also the time of my life when my best friend was Jimmy Gordon. Our favorite play-place was the field between his house and mine. It spanned about 10 acres and was only seldom mowed. We did everything in that field, from catching baby rabbits with our baseball gloves to playing army. One army adventure stands out in my mind. We decided to build an underground secret cabin, so we all began to shovel the dirt to create a nice pit, about four feet round and four feet deep. Then we covered the pit with long sticks, then shorter ones until we could uproot grass and hide it really well. It was not that pleasant or roomy inside, so we decided that this was our anti-tank pit and part-time cabin.

My neighbor seldom mowed that field as I said, so imagine our surprise when one Saturday he was out there with his riding mower going at it. The grass was so high that he had to set his mowing deck as high as it would go to make the first cut. We liked the neighbor, but didn't know what to do, as he cut closer and closer to the anti-tank pit. We finally decided it would be better if we weren't in the area if the worst happened. Well. The worst happened, proving that we were very effective anti-tank-pit diggers. Imagine his surprise, just riding along and then...whump!

I truly wanted to do the right thing and confess. I wanted to...but I never did. Only if that good neighbor reads this book will he find out who trapped his riding lawn mower that day. I did find out that he wasn't hurt, and I thanked God for that, but quickly said "amen" before God had the opportunity to say anything to me about confessing. I can almost picture and hear St. Peter at the gate saying, "Rick, it looks good, but what about that matter of the anti-lawn-mower pit?" I thank God for His grace, because since I am 57 years old, that neighbor is likely passed away and it's too late to confess to him. Have I checked if he's still around? Nope!

I do keep my speed down in Pennsylvania, however, for fear the officer checks my license and comes back with, "There's a 47 year old warrant for your arrest for reckless lawnmower endangerment and criminal trespass. Mr. Watt. I'll have to take you in."

INSIGHT ONE: Don't we do dumb things when we're kids? A lot of those things were so dangerous that it's a wonder we made it to adulthood. Other things were so dumb that it's a wonder nobody beat us senseless. As we get older, we should begin to realize the consequences of our actions to others, including our own family. A stupid mistake can make us responsible for someone else getting hurt, like drinking and driving. We need to make sure our mistakes don't hurt others.

When we think of some of the dangerous things we did as kids, it's a wonder we survived. Yep, so now we can stop our children from making those same stupid mistakes, right? Well, we can try.

INSIGHT TWO: The simplicity with which we enjoyed things as a child can be lost as we grow older. It makes no sense that a bunch of kids had such fun digging with shovels until they were sweaty and filthy, but we had a blast! If our parents had forced us to help dig a septic tank, we would have whined. **What would happen if we decided ahead-of-time to enjoy any hard work that was going to benefit us in the end?** Can you imagine your wife watching and listening as you gleefully dig a septic tank by hand, singing all the time? She'd think you were nuts, but you'd be a happy nut!

Mark 10:15: I tell you the truth, anyone who will not receive the kingdom of God like a little child will never enter it.

CHAPTER NINE:
MY HUNTING BUDDY, DAVE

David was my opposite. He could weld, do diesel and gasoline mechanics, do plumbing, electrical and construction work, paint a car with proficiency, and generally was a uniquely talented person. I can change my oil on my car, paint a house, and drive my car to a mechanic to be fixed. I met Dave one Sunday at the church I was pastoring in Tuscaloosa, Alabama. He was an honest, hard-working man and not really religious.

Well, David got tricked into coming to my church one Sunday when his sister-in-law promised Dave's two daughters to take the family to McDonald's afterward if they'd come. They came, but the chip on Dave's shoulder was the size of a fireplace log. In a couple of weeks, God got a really talented member and worker for His church.

David couldn't read well. I began to stop every day where David maintained the 7Up and Dr. Pepper truck fleet. Every lunchtime I'd find him in his mechanic's office for lunch, eating and reading his Bible. Every day! Now the Bible is not that easy to read, but Dave had a hunger and a determination, and he was determined to read the Bible and learn what it had to say to him. Once he read it, David lived it.

One thing that I didn't mention is that Dave is the ultimate outdoorsman, and I am a hunter, as well. We began to share that hobby and our friendship grew. As a pastor, I could be myself with Dave, even if I was struggling, and David was the same with me. He was my main prayer-friend when I wrestled with church junk or got discouraged.

As David began to read more, an opening came with the Junior High Boys Sunday School Class. Those of you who have ever taught Middle School boys are already praying for Dave as you read this. Those are rowdy kids, and ours were especially rowdy. So, Dave went in there to teach them and could hardly read. He'd read something and several kids would snicker because the kids could read much better than he could. After about 2 weeks the snickering had stopped and kids volunteered to read. He loved them, and they could tell it. They loved him back. Not one kid dared to snicker when Dave read, or the wrath of God's Junior High Boys Class fell upon them after church.

Dave's reading improved amazingly, however. One day he told me, "Bro, I'd like to preach sometime." I had every confidence in Dave, but I was afraid of what the attitudes and responses of the people in the congregation would be. I said yes and set a date for a Sunday evening service time and the whole church showed up. David did some reading and it was pretty good, but then he shared his heart and his story of coming to Jesus. *(By the way, one reason the attendance was good was that the Junior High boys made their parents come.)* David has taught in many situations and preached many times since then. He was always intelligent and talented, but he has added to his list of abilities, being a wonderful example of a growing, sharing, genuine Christian who really reads well.

INSIGHT ONE: People can grow! Not only were people amazed by the growth and the sermon of Dave's, but I'm sure that David and his own family were amazed as well. A lot of us could say, "I've never done that...yet," and we'd realize that there are still things to learn and to do that will be wonderful when we accept the challenge. **One of the best ways God shows His love and power is by transforming someone's life right before our eyes.**

INSIGHT TWO: The world is full of friends you've never met. Dave and I were very different from each other, yet we made great encouragers in each other's lives. Yes, we've had arguments and even been upset with each other, but our commitment to the friendship is stronger than our commitment to some stupid argument. We have now been hunting together for more than 24 years. I return to Tuscaloosa to join him every year. **Don't miss a wonderful blessing of God by not seeking new people for friends in your life.**

INSIGHT THREE: There is a thing called the "halo effect" that makes others blind to our faults as they concentrate on the "halo." The halo is the stuff that's so good, that people either intentionally or unintentionally forget the flaws. Love is the greatest halo of all. **If you know you're loaded with faults, just load up more heavily on love, and people (most people) can ignore the faults**. Look for the halo on others, and you'll soon find it easier to love imperfect people and ignore their faults, as well.

Ecclesiastes 4:10: If one falls down, his friend can help him up. But pity the man who falls and has no one to help him up!

CHAPTER TEN:
OUR FIRST ADULT CABIN

They say that grown men are just little boys with more expensive toys. Maybe so, because the joy that came from building cabins and clubhouses out of junk when I was a little guy did not diminish when I became a very big guy.

Bob Baumhower of the "Miami Dolphin's Killer B's" had a plantation near Eutaw, Alabama, that he and his parents, Bob Sr. and Patti, shared. Bob and Patti attended the Church that I pastored, and it happened that David Smelley and I became the only two guys allowed to hunt deer there, except for family and a great number of pro-football players. In fact, Bob allowed us to renovate an old slave-quarters on the back of the property into our hunting camp. It couldn't have been super-old because it was made of old-time concrete block, but the roof leaked and the weeds had overgrown it. A Weedeater and sling blades took care of the weeds. A plastic liner fixed the roof. Inside we installed a gas oven and a wood burning stove made from an old Dr. Pepper syrup barrel. We built two sets of queen-sized bunks in one room that resulted in wall-to-wall beds. We scrubbed the walls and floor and laid down some old carpet pieces. Dave ran electric wire and switches so that we could hook up a car battery and 12 volt light bulbs for light. Our wives were appalled, but we felt this was luxury-in-our-own minds. All the cabin-joy of younger years returned. Building the cabin was so fulfilling, but there was more fun to come.

It was so pitch-black at night that we'd have a snack, read our Bibles by the dim light, begin a conversation, move to our bunk beds and fall asleep talking. How long did that take? Oh, we were asleep by 9:30pm because of the darkness and no TV. I wonder how many of us would go to bed earlier if it wasn't for our TV, and wake up rested? Well, sometimes in the middle of the night we'd be awakened by the pitter-patter of little rat feet on the beams above us, but they never really bothered us. We put out some poison and never panicked. That story didn't sit well with our wives, though. They really weren't interested in spending the night there. Dave and I would awaken at about 3:30am, rested, ready to go. There was the tasty breakfast, the many warm clothes (depending upon the season) and off we'd go out the door to some of the best deer hunting in Alabama.

INSIGHT ONE: Work is fun when you have the picture of the end result in mind before you start. That's called "vision." The thing is already real before you begin to build it. Working with Dave was great, because he could do anything. If there was something weird that "couldn't be done," my A.D.D. mind could find a way, explain it, and Dave could make it reality. That's the beauty of teamwork. No one is looking for credit, and everyone is working for success. If families, businesses, neighborhoods, and churches would learn to put aside the power-struggles and the need for credit, God would bless us with happier and more productive lives.

INSIGHT TWO: What other people might regard as junk can be your treasure. That's why garage sales work. The trick is matching up the person with the right treasure or the right job. I loved our little cabin, and I treasure the many years we enjoyed because of the generosity of the Baumhowers. We got to meet a lot of pro-football players, but among the greatest joys was sleeping warmly in that dark cabin, listening to the pitter patter of little rat feet.

INSIGHT THREE: This really belongs with insight two, but it is so important that I wanted it to have its own spot. Here it is. Don't miss it. It can change your life...

MANY TIMES, HAPPINESS COMES MORE FROM WANTING WHAT WE HAVE THAN FROM HAVING WHAT WE WANT!

Don't waste time longing for things you don't have and ignoring the blessings you do have. I meet men all the time who have been unfaithful to their wives, pursuing something they think they need, rather than enriching what they already have. So many of them are now divorced and tell me, "Rick, I was so stupid. I had it made and I didn't know it. Now it's too late." Maybe it would be good to take a piece of paper right now and make a list of good things in our lives, good things about our wife and kids, good things about our job. We may discover things we have overlooked for a long time.

GOOD THINGS IN MY LIFE:

Our First Adult Cabin

Some other guys never give effort to the relationship they have. They just go hunting and fishing and expect "the wife" to keep the tribe, hold down the fort, and be there with supper cooked, waiting for them when they get home, and of course thinking their "woman" was just anticipating a wonderful reunion in the marriage bed. Some of those guys think everything is great until their wife asks for a divorce.

Our guns need cleaning and oiling, the cabin needs cleaning, the feedlots need planting, the oil in the car needs changing, but somehow the wife doesn't need anything except to be handed the paycheck? **Are we so dumb that we never maintain, build, or encourage the woman who shares our life?** Stop and think how much she means to your life and actually think about ways to make her feel the same way about you in her life. When did you last serve and build her? Never call her your "old lady." What does that make you?

Matthew 6:21 and Luke 12:34: For where your treasure is, there will your heart be also.
(Translation: See where you are applying and investing yourself, and you'll know what you consider to be the most important.)

CHAPTER ELEVEN:
WHEN THE RATS TAKE OVER

One weekend before deer season, Dave and I went to our cabin on the Baumhower Plantation to get it ready for the big weekend. There was no big deal, just clean up a bit, air it out, make the beds with fresh sheets, weed-eat around the doors and windows and check the roof for leaks. We didn't count on rats; Dave startled them when he opened the door and they ran everywhere.

"What was that?" I asked. "Rats, Bro (Bro is my nickname), get a stick." We each got a stick, but Dave didn't realize a childhood fear I had. A farmer once told me about a rat running up his pant-leg. I got a stick, but I was thinking rats-in-my-underwear biting me you-know-where. We jumped into the cabin like Butch Cassidy and the Sundance kid jumping out of that house surrounded by the Mexican army. No karate expert could have been more precise. With my pant legs in mind, I did not miss one rat as I swung that stick with precision. If there was a Rat Kung Fu Hall of Fame, I'd be in it.

Dave had moved straight ahead and I had stayed right by the door *(in case I had to run for help, of course)*. I personally killed 16 rats with my faithful rat-stick. There was not a rat moving when we were finished. We found out that they had built a nest in the box springs of one of our queen-sized double beds. We pulled that box spring out of there and put the mattress back on the solid sheet of plywood below. We had a rat-shoveling party and cleaned up a lot of rat residue. Everything got a thorough scrubbing, because no rat was going to keep us from our faithful rounds with the deer herd in the coming weekend. We must have done an incredible (also amazingly quick and athletic) job of removing the rats, because there was no pitter patter of little feet on the rafters on that first night of the season (and I was listening). I could just imagine a horror movie made about us, "Revenge of the Rats," when our rat-chewed bodies were found.

INSIGHT ONE: You never know when some rat will step in and mess things up, whether it's trespassing hunters on your leased land or a landowner who decides to lease to someone else. Sometimes you just have to handle things and play with the hand you're dealt. In this situation, there was no choice. We didn't hate the rats, we were just protecting our underwear...'er, I mean our cabin. Our goal was to have the cabin ready, and that meant the sideline of getting rid of the rats.

If you look at the problems of your life like rats, here's the lineup. You are not here to deal with rats. You have a bigger job to do (ours was getting the cabin ready). Don't focus upon the rats. Focus upon the goal and the rats become simply an obstacle to obtaining your goal. **When the goal is in mind, the problems along the way simply have to be dealt with in order to move closer to the goal.** When the rats (problems) become the goal, they can overwhelm you. Don't let the problems of life take your eyes off the big picture, the goal ahead. Some people spend their whole lives swatting rats and mosquitoes. God put you here for much more than that.

INSIGHT TWO: Read insight one and begin to apply it to your marriage and family. **If you focus on the "problems" in your marriage and family, they can take your eyes off the fact that in a service of worship called a marriage ceremony, you promised to God and to this woman to keep her a priority in your life.** Let's face it guys, sometimes she is so consistent and regular in what she does for us that we forget to be grateful. Sometimes when the problems come and we've taken her "good stuff" for granted, the problems become the focus, and we forget the good stuff until the relationship is ruined and irreparable. By then she no longer sees anything worth fixing.

Guys, if it's more sex you want, you are tuned in to the minds of 90% of guys in this world. The other guys are just as dumb as we are. We want more lovin' from our wives, but we can't make a withdrawal from the bank when we haven't made any deposits earlier. If we do, that's called a loan and it comes with "big interest" for you to pay and "little interest" on her part. **A successful man with reasonable intelligence wants the woman he loves to be happy.** Invest some attention and encouragement in her.

By the way, if you are offended that I'm talking about sex, let's face it, it's on a guy's mind. According to my Bible, God invented it for married people to enjoy, including all the plumbing required. If you can't handle it, forget what you already read and just go on and read the next chapter.

1 Corinthians 9:24: Do you not know that in a race all the runners run, but only one gets the prize? Run in such a way as to get the prize. (PS- If we win the rat-race, does that make us the biggest rat? What do we win?)

CHAPTER TWELVE:
BRO'S BARBECUE TRAILER

Since I was meeting Dave Smelley for lunch nearly every day to mentor and visit and pray and share, we also did a lot of dreaming. One day I saw the back end of a Dr. Pepper drink truck that was badly rusted out and sitting there in what appeared to be the truck graveyard. You've seen them hauling Coke or Pepsi, with their roll-up-and-down aluminum shutter sides. Well, this one didn't have a truck; it was just the bed with the roll-downs. "Y'know, Dave," I said, "that would make a great trailer to build a smoking box on the back and make the inside into a processing and serving place...our own business—a bbq trailer!

We could use the roll-down doors to secure the windows over the screens we would build in. We could sandblast it (correction, David could sandblast it, 'cause I don't know anything about how to do that) and then paint it Bama colors, crimson and white (we were in Tuscaloosa, Alabama, home of the UA Crimson Tide) and build a deck on the tongue to have another service window with a red and white canopy overtop. Now, that was a lot of talkin,' but I was painting a mental picture and Dave was seeing it, too. He added, "We can put a gas starter in the firebox on the back and have shelves in the smoker that open into the inside." So, we went to the owner and he said, "If you get it out of here, it's yours."

So began our project. I was the grunt worker, and Dave provided all the skill. When we'd hit a roadblock, we'd acknowledge that I'm not skilled, and then he'd ask me how to solve the problem. Since I wasn't in the paradigm, I was usually able to suggest something (from ADD land) that would light his creative brain afire and on we'd go. There was quite an amount of money involved, including metal for the firebox and smoker, angle iron for rails, wood decking for the floor, paint for the body, window frames and screen, a stove, double glass-front Dr. Pepper refrigerator (rescued from the fridge graveyard), stainless steel countertops with legs (they just magically appeared in the junkyard one day and were given to us), and that red and white canopy. In a couple months, we had a masterpiece. She was 28 feet long and 8 feet wide and impressive. It was like playing with a giant erector set for two overgrown boys...and I know that you know what I mean. (I can't wait to have grandkids so I can play with Lincoln Logs again.)

My nickname was Bro and I was already pretty well known for my slow-smoked meats and special-made barbecue sauce. Now we had Dave and Bro's BBQ wagon. I can seriously say that it was impressive. We got a license and sold smoked bbq outside the stadium at Bama Football Games. We did quite well with our little side experiment. You could find us at horseshows, business picnics, and just set up along the road. Occasionally, Sonny's BBQ would rent it from us to do a job.

When I left for Boca Raton, I knew that my new area would not respond well to a BBQ wagon. We put it up for sale and sold it to Bobby Baumhower's Wings Restaurant. I still think back to the project and smile.

INSIGHT ONE: Some of the greatest experiences in our lives have come to an end. It was sad to leave Dave and the wagon in Tuscaloosa. There was a time of mourning, but we've got to get up and build new memories. **I knew other excitement was ahead. It has been! It still is!**

INSIGHT TWO: One way to know that good stuff is ahead when leaving something wonderful behind is that you learn to create the good stuff in your mind as you move forward. **If you and your creative juices did it once, can't you do it again? Vision keeps our life exciting!**

INSIGHT THREE: Moving forward means sacrifice. I was also leaving the best hunting I have ever seen. The memories were rich, the hunts were successful, and here I was moving to Boca Raton, Florida, to the land of sophistication. My kids were saddened that they were leaving the only home they'd ever known and all their friends and the church we'd grown to love. It was time for Dad (me) to inject some excitement. I couldn't fake it, so I had to do some searching within myself and realized, "I can't live my life driving forward, while looking out the back window." Looking backward can bring on a big crash, and I realized that I wasn't the only one in the car of my life. I thanked God for all the good I'd found in Tuscaloosa, Alabama, and then I thanked Him for all He had for me in Boca Raton, Florida, where we found another wonderful adventure. I wrote a song in my head about "Goin' On to Boca Raton," taught it to Marsha and the kids, and we sang it all the way to Boca.

*Hebrews 12:1: Therefore, since we are surrounded by such a great cloud of witnesses,
let us throw off everything that hinders and the sin that so easily entangles,
and let us run with perseverance the race marked out for us.
Philippians 3:13-14: ...Forgetting those things that are behind and straining toward what is ahead,
I press on toward the goal to win the prize for which God has called us heavenward in Christ Jesus.*

CHAPTER THIRTEEN:
TACKLE BASKETBALL

I'm not bragging when I say that my son, Chris, inherited my talent for basketball. On a scale of one to ten, I was a "3" in a new game called tackle basketball and a total "zero" at real basketball. I always fouled out. This body was just not made to play basketball. I truly believe that God said, "Let's build this one with a gift for preaching. Oops, no room for basketball talent. Oh well. OK, boys, let's get this one on his way." So my son inherited defective basketball genes.

I would like to say that when I was 11, I was a better basketball player than Michael Jordan...but that was the year Michael was born, and I know I was better than a newborn. Just to let you know how bad I am, I think Jordan could have beaten me by his first birthday.

Chris attended an amazing Christian School in Boca (Boca Raton Christian School) and decided to join the basketball team. I applauded his motivation, but worried for his success. He was obviously among the least talented guys on his team because his dad had neglected to teach him how to play basketball. (I didn't know how to do it right. Give me a break, here. How can you teach your son what you can't do?) Chris put his all into it and was allowed in for several short moments at the end of each game. Then one game the team had an excessive number of fouls and Chris was the only one left to send in. I prayed fervently, "Oh God, don't let them throw him the ball. Be merciful to my son, O' Lord." The other team moved down the court and Chris reached in for the steal, got the ball, dribbled a bit, and passed to his open man, who scored. He kept doing that again and again, and his own team began to pass to him. He never shot once, but he made the right pass every time. It was amazing to watch Chris take the ball from the other team's players. The coach just stood there in total shock, and my wife and I screamed like crazy people, growing hoarse with yelling and excitement.

About a month later, we were at the awards banquet for all sports of the school. It was a nice-sized school, with full programs in every sport. Basketball awards came, with the announcement "MOST

IMPROVED PLAYER–CHRIS WATT." I listened to the coach retell the story. We were so proud, more so because it was all great effort on his part and had nothing to do with casual, natural ability.

About a year before that, Chris had gone out for flag football. I threw with him often, as I had a great arm (well, I got the football gene), and I understood the game. Still, Chris was young and though he could catch, it was mostly if the ball hit him in the chest. In the first game of his first season, I didn't realize what his coach had done. If I'd realized, I'd have warned him to perhaps practice with Chris a little more first. Our quarterback dropped back and threw a 15-yard floating pass to the receiver running down the sideline. The receiver leapt into the air like he was a deer on wings to grab that overthrown pass and moved another five yards down the field before they pulled his flag. It was Chris. Our Chris!

INSIGHT ONE: Don't underestimate your kids. They'll surprise you in many ways. Just about the time you give up, they'll amaze you. I'm not just talking sports, but business, responsibility, discipline. That kid who has to be pulled out of bed to go to school, who gets teacher notes about not doing his homework, could grow up to be governor. Have you changed since you were a kid? So can he/she.

Never let your child see you give up on him/her. Seeing that can make them quickly give up on themselves, as well. Sow the seeds of encouragement, even when they feel they can't succeed. The seeds you sow will grow. Which ones will you sow?

INSIGHT TWO: Everyone isn't made to be a star, but we can all have our "star plays" to remember. I won't forget either game mentioned above, but neither will I let my son forget. I'm not just proud of him when he's great. I'm proud when he's simply himself.

INSIGHT THREE: What would happen if, when you have memory flashbacks like this, you took a moment to write a short note to the school that made it possible and thank them? What if you wrote a note to your child, reminding him of a great moment in his life? I have gotten notes from former friends that thrill me and remind me that I have occasionally found my moments to shine. **Remember your good moments and help others remember or create theirs.**

2 Corinthians 9:6: Remember this: Whoever sows sparingly will also reap sparingly,
and whoever sows generously will also reap generously.

CHAPTER FOURTEEN:
THE WORLD'S WORST DOLPHIN FISHERMAN...ME!

Some men are fishermen and others are just men who fish. I am the latter. I would call myself a hunter, but I am a poor fisherman. If they aren't biting in the first hour, I'm ready to go home, especially if the boat is miles out in the Atlantic and the boat has no air conditioning. I guess I'd say that I fish, but I'm not truly a fisherman.

Don't think it's sad when I say I'm not truly a fisherman. I can laugh at my own antics and still feel good about myself. I know what I'm good at. I just really, really know what I stink at and floating in the deep sea is one of those things. So, I've learned to laugh because I can't be excellent at everything. It may help other guys who are feeling low, if they see that being bad at something doesn't make a person inferior. It just makes you normal. Just excel where you are gifted.

Do you know what you call the high school computer nerd four years after high school? You call him "boss." Y'see, no one is good at everything, but you can be excellent at something else. New talents can emerge all through your life. What's that you're saying? You're great at everything? Well, you just keep on believing that little buddy. When you get married, your wife and kids will bring you back to reality.

There were several times when Bill Jerrils took us out in his boat from Fort Lauderdale, Florida, that we got into a school of dolphin. This is a fish and not like Flipper. We caught fish all morning long. He'd look for the weed-line or something floating on the water and we'd fish around it. It wasn't unusual to catch 30 or more fish. After the big haul, we'd head back to port and I'd be thrilled with the experience. It was the days that Bill was not fish-tuned that were hard for me.

Fishing had been fun before, but it suddenly turned into a scorching sauna with no relief. No amount of drink would cool me down or quench my salt-flavored, parched throat. The guys just watched those fishing poles as we drifted around looking for a weed-line or a floating board. The cabin actually felt hotter than the direct sun, so there was no escape. A migraine set in, my stomach churned and sometimes I fed the fish over the side of the boat. My neck muscles would tighten up so that swallowing was difficult. Meanwhile, the other guys seemed fine, and I didn't want to ruin their time. I'd occasionally slip into the hotbox called a cabin and lay on the cushions of the seat down there, sweating more because of being sick than hot...but it was a close contest. Moaning seemed to help until the moan ended. "We'll find fish soon," I heard Bill say to the other guys. I had ceased to believe in such miracles. I didn't care about fish anymore.

The thought of miracles made me think about turning to God, but first I had to hit the side of the boat and feed the fish again. The other friends began to call me "chum." You fishermen will understand the terminology. It was also a miracle that there was anything left inside me to come out over the side of the boat. I watched carefully for kidneys and other essential internal body parts. Oh, yeah, I was going to pray, so here goes: "Oh God who loves me, don't let me suffer like this. Take me home to heaven right now where it's cool and shady. My aching brain can stay behind and you can give me another one that doesn't hurt like this. Oh yeah, I could use a new stomach, too. This one is turning inside out and hurts beyond belief. Oh, by the way, when you give me that new body I'm supposed to get in heaven, I'd like a six-pack of muscles where my stomach is. It seems my six-pack has become a keg in the last couple of years. So I'm ready Lord, take me home now."

Then the worst thing that could have happened, happened. One of the guys caught a fish. That meant we'd be here longer. "That's not funny, God. I know you have a sense of humor, but I can't take any more." Funny thing, after a few minutes with no bites one of the guys said, "Let's go in. I have to do some things this afternoon." They all agreed and we began the longest ride of my life back to the shore. Once in a while I'd hang over the side, just to make memories for the other guys. They'd need some stories to laugh about in the future.

INSIGHT ONE: Some guys fish and others are fishermen. Being on a boat with a fishing pole doesn't make me a fisherman any more than being in my garage makes me a car. Some guys enjoy fishing and others live for it. The same is true for hunting, and even for parenting. Some guys make each of these a fulfilling career, while others do it like an occasional necessity.

INSIGHT TWO: If you don't fish, you're not a fisherman. Imagine a guy fishing and just having a relaxing time. He has leaned back in his comfortable fishing seat and pulled the bass boat into the shade, where his eyes are half-closed and dreamland is quickly approaching. Then some stupid fish bites on his hook and he'll have to play it, reel it in, and even bend over and remove it from the hook. What a terrible interruption of a great fishing day. Funny? Maybe, but that guy is not a real fisherman. He just fishes.

If Jesus said we'd be fishers-of-men when we follow Him, are we really Christians if we don't fish? Was Jesus right or wrong when He said that? He's right? Well, are you a fisher-of-men or a sitter in the boat? I'm wondering if you can follow Christ without fishing for men. Jesus didn't seem to think so.

INSIGHT THREE: The other guys in the boat were having fun even without catching fish. I was the only one miserable. Ever been there? This reminds me of the times I hear folks complain about things they think are important, while most every one of the gang is actually excited and involved in the fun and encouraging lives all around them. The miserable guy calls out, "Hey, everything stops until I get my way, my kind of activities, and credit for all I do."

Have you ever heard someone in the Outback Restaurant complain because he's not being fed? The truth is, **they're not supposed to feed you. They are just to bring out the food and make it available.** You use the silverware, cut the bites, chew the food, and swallow. Yet we all hear people in churches gripe, "I'm not being fed." Ditto to the above.

So, if folks are having fun and I'm chumming over the side of the boat, I need to pray to see the good stuff that's going on and enjoy it… or get out of the boat and find a boat that is run like I want. **I never want to stand in the way of ways God is blessing or discourage others who are enjoying life.**

INSIGHT FOUR: We men like things our way. We want to be king of our castle. Sometimes everyone else is happy except us. Who is right? **One of the things I have realized in life is** (and please don't spread this around to all the thousands of people who think I'm perfect) **that sometimes I'm wrong.** Yep, me! It's inevitable. If I have not learned all that there is to learn, then there are probably some things I now believe that are incorrect. Now, I do stand up for what I believe, except when God shows me I'm wrong, and then it's time to bow down, confess, and receive the new stuff. We can't be right until we realize the wrong and get right. A real man admits he's wrong because he wants to be right.

You are not just responsible to provide food and lodging for your home. You provide motivation and encouragement, fulfillment and love. God made you the leader of your home, just as He wants to be the Priest and Provider for your family. If you've surrendered that job to your wife, to let her be the religious leader for your kids, then look again. I'm not encouraging you to be religious. I'm encouraging you to acknowledge God and His wisdom and ask for more and more of it. I'm saying that leading means going in the way you want those who follow you to go. We men like to be good at what we do. So why not be a better husband and father? God is ready to help us with that and show us where we need to change to be even better than we are now.

Many guys think being a man-of-faith is sissy stuff. Others think it's all guilt-driven living. The perception that some preachers give is that GOD IS UP THERE WITH A BIG FLY SWATTER, READY TO SQUASH YOUR SINFUL HEAD WITH A SINGLE SWIPE! That is just wrong. Preachers who go that way have given an impression that keeps most men out of church, because we know what sinners we are. We know the lustful thoughts we have. We know the insecurities we have while we're pretending we're tough guys who have it all together. God is your friend, dude. He made you on purpose. **Some of us are ashamed of the job we're doing as a husband and dad, but God is right there like the greatest coach in the world, saying,**

"Boy, you've got the stuff. You just need to learn how to tune and focus it. I know you've got the stuff, 'cause I put it there. You just haven't found it yet.
Let me help and you'll be the man I made you to be in every situation. I'm your fan, man. I'm wanting to make you a winner. Will you let me?"–God

If you've never heard anything like that about God before, it's about time you did. I'm speaking to you guys who get drunk every weekend because you think that "numb beats dumb" and you feel like a failure. God didn't make a mistake when He made you. He made you on purpose and for a purpose. You don't even need a preacher to help you find God. He's been pursuing your friendship all your life, just excited about the two of you knowing each other better. You won't get it all at once, but how cool will it be to know that when you fall, God is there to pick you up. How great will it be on the day you're ready to eat and see the look on your wife and children's face when you say,

"How about I pray for this meal? 'God, bless this food and my family, and help me be a better dad and husband. In Jesus' name, Amen.'"

I'd love to be there when you say that prayer, to catch your wife as she falls out of her chair.

John 3:17: For God did not send his Son into the world to condemn the world, but to save the world through him.

CHAPTER FIFTEEN:
LOST IN RACCOON LAND

It was my first raccoon hunt in Oklahoma, near Bartlesville. The season was winter and cold, but there was no snow on the ground. I took out my Kawasaki street-and-trail bike and thought that was the way to go, leaving the car for my wife. Troy was an avid coon hunter with several great coon hounds. He lived about 20 miles east of Bartlesville and the ride was nice as I made my way there at 9pm and 60mph. His dogs were ready and so was I, so we hit the woods. Before long those hounds were baying "treed, treed" in dog language and Troy was hustling through the dark woods. I was a young guy, so I could keep up pretty well wearing a head-mount flashlight. There were three coons in that tree and Troy didn't kill them because he wanted them around for another hunt. We set off in a different direction to find more coons.

Soon the dogs hit another trail and Troy could tell where they were and what progress they were making by their barks. I had no reason to doubt him, so I just gave the old "uh huh" and kept running. I don't know to this day if Troy was kidding or not, but around 12:30am he stopped and said, "I've not been this far before, and I'm not sure where we are." I resisted the urge to say, "You're kidding, right?" and just said, "Your house is that way," pointing in the direction I felt was correct.

I've always had this unique sense of direction. Maybe it's because of my ADD that I'm tuned in with my own GPS, but Troy said, "OK," and we headed that way for about ½ hour. Suddenly he stopped and turned to me, saying, "This is the Buellers' fence; you were right." I acted like "of course I'm right." We men have to act that way. It's in our genes to pretend we know what we're doing, right? (It's like when we open the hood of our broken-down car and go, "mmm hmmm," but really have no idea what's wrong under there.) It started to really snowstorm and blow, but 20 minutes later we were back at Troy's house.

I got on my trail-bike and cranked her up, thanked Troy, and headed home. I wanted to get home before it got worse. Little did I know that my adventure was just beginning.

INSIGHT ONE: We often trust our lives into the hands of people we don't know very well. Troy was my guide, but I knew little about him. Sometimes we get into cars without really knowing the driver that well. We go to a church and listen to a preacher, trusting he knows what he's talking about. We get into a plane and don't really know whether the pilot has a hangover. We get a Yahoo map online and follow it, not knowing if they've updated; or we may have typed one wrong number leading us to Lower Slobovia. **Maybe we should be a little more aware of following people without thinking about it first.**

INSIGHT TWO: When I traveled to Honduras for a mission trip, I saw a young man in one school that all the girls were watching. His team-mates also depended upon his direction. After the game I went to him and through a translator, asked him if he realized that he had a gift of leadership, and that the other kids were following him. He answered "Yes." Then I asked, "Where will you lead them?" There is more to this story, but the important part to you and for me is that there are some people (kids, adults, friends) who are looking to us for leadership. If we are negative, we will lead them into negativity. If we are positive, perhaps somewhere positive. If we are selfish, we will lead them for our own benefit. If not, we will try to lead them for theirs. **Do some people follow you? Where will you lead them?**

INSIGHT THREE: It's fun to wander and explore, but we need to remember the way home. One man was asked if he was lost when a group of hunters found him in the woods. "No," he said, "I'm not really trying to go anywhere in particular, so how could I be lost?" Truth is, men, if you have no direction, you need to realize you are lost. Men need goals, direction, vision, a plan. We need to know where home is. Some of you are struggling with that direction. Where's home? It's a good idea to find someone who knows in order to get proper direction. I suggest prayer to God.

1 John 3:7: Dear children, do not let anyone lead you astray
He who does what is right is righteous, just as he is righteous.

CHAPTER SIXTEEN:
AFTER THE COON HUNT– THE MOTORCYLE SNOW STORM

After hunting raccoon with Troy, I jumped on my Kawasaki to rush home before the snowstorm became too bad. Too late. I should have stayed at Troy's house or had him drive me home. My clothing was inadequate, the snow was pounding my face right under my shield, the wind made my zippered jacket feel like it was open. The wind also pushed me toward the ditch and I constantly battled it. Tears were running down my face from the cold in my eyes and pain took hold where it was just cold before. I thought about stopping at one of the farmhouses every 4 miles or so, but it was after 12:30am, and they would be terrified by the frozen man on their porch. I pushed on.

Only 20 more miles to Bartlesville and I could warm up at a Denny's Restaurant (they were open all night). Then I realized there was no Denny's on my path. I thought about dying in the snow. Dumb? Maybe, but when you're in that kind of pain you think about sliding into the ditch, being knocked unconscious and freezing to death. I saw my funeral in my imagination and the pastor warning the congregation about the foolishness of going into the blizzard of life on the wrong vehicle with the wrong clothing, immortalizing me as a really stupid young man.

I tried to stop thinking morbidly. I thought, "Hey, if I'm hurting, that means I'm not frozen numb yet!" Oh, yeah that really helped a lot. I wanted to tell whoever said that to shut up, but I was the only guy there and I needed me to keep talking to keep me awake. I started talking to myself out loud. Then I tried singing. My speedometer said 30 but I felt like it was 60 in that wind and snow hitting me like little bb's. The sign said I was just five miles from Bartlesville. "Come on, Rick, you've done 15 miles. You can do another five." I wanted to tell him, "shut up" again, but he was me. I began singing again. The shivering made a strange vibrato in my voice. My lower jaw was doing that thing that lower jaws do when you're really cold. The farm and ranch houses were far apart and it would have felt better to see signs of life, lights in windows, cars in driveways. When I did see signs of life, it encouraged me.

"If I freeze in this sitting position while riding this bike", I thought, "how will they get my body into a casket?" Don't laugh at me, guys. Oh, go ahead and laugh. I began to think of my wife at my funeral. Now the tears were both from the pain of the cold and from the sympathy for poor me. I thought, "Maybe I'll find a policeman and I can warm-up in his car. No policeman to be found? Oh look, Bartlesville, now turn right and on to Dewey where my house is."

Suddenly, it was the final run. Another 3 miles remained, but it was 3 miles of familiar places, restaurants (closed), the mall, the places I picked up kids when I ran the Sunday van route. Oh, there's our house and the light's on. I can kick snow away to open the garage and put the cycle in. I can hardly get the key in the lock because I'm shaking, but the door is open and the warmth almost hurts as it hits me. Marsha fell asleep on the couch, waiting for me and then met me at the door. I made it. I'm home!

INSIGHT ONE: Endurance is amazing. Sometimes it can outperform ability. I love the movie "Rudy." Watch it sometime with your kids. He seemingly doesn't have the size or ability of the starting players, but he gives his all on the practice team. The coach has already closed his mind to giving him a chance. Rudy wants to play for Notre Dame. In the last game of the season of his last year, the teammates make certain that he plays and Rudy makes the tackles. It's a great story of endurance and persistence.

INSIGHT TWO: Sometimes we have no idea what we can do until we have to do it. The phrase "do or die" comes to mind. Don't underestimate yourself or anyone else. God put stuff in you that you haven't discovered yet. That's one of the amazing challenges of life. When the going gets tough...keep on. (You didn't really expect me to say what you anticipated, did you?) Why not? Because sometimes when the going gets tough, the weak get strong and rise to the occasion. If that's where you are in life, rise up!

INSIGHT THREE: There is scripture that tells us that God won't allow us to face more than we can handle without at least making a way for us to escape. **Some of the junk I've gone through in life makes me think that God has a lot more confidence in me than I do.** Truth is, He does. You too! He made us, and He knows what He put in there. He's helped me do things that I was amazed at, because I knew I couldn't do it alone. You too, dude! There's stuff in you that you haven't discovered yet. Sometimes we wait far too long to find out what we can handle, and we're surprised. So, go surprise yourself.

After the Coon Hunt–The Motorcyle Snow Storm

Philippians 4:13: I can do everything through him who gives me strength.

CHAPTER SEVENTEEN:
OUR NEW CABIN

The best cabin we ever built is the one we have now. It is made of Styrofoam panels that are sealed in solid aluminum sheets on both sides and put together with channel and metal screws. The floor is even heavier styrofoam, designed to support weight and be a roof. The roof is also the heavy styro, sealed in aluminum. I bought the cabin piece by piece from PGT Industries in Nokomis, Florida.

The materials were made to build extra rooms on a house and are hurricane resistant. When they had any damaged panels, a friend called me and I'd go down with Jim Hawkins and his big trailer to pick 'em up. Sometimes they didn't even charge me. Mostly they made the cost reasonable. I also picked up the aluminum angle and channel that was too bent to use for a first-rate job. Good ol' Jim's airplane hangar was full of that stuff for a while. The aluminum and styro came in 4x10 and 4x14 sheets.

I began to engineer the building. (I am not an engineer.) I took my results to some folks at PGT's engineering department and they told me it looked OK. When I had sufficient parts (about a 1 year process) I rented a U-Haul truck and headed to Bama (about 12 hours in a rental truck) from my home in Sarasota, Florida. There I met David Smelley, my best huntin' buddy, and we drove to the land that he and his brothers had leased, where we unloaded and tarped it all. It took David, Wayne, and Nicky awhile to get the floor together, but soon we had walls up and the roof in place for a 16x34 building with an eight by four bathroom sticking out from it. The cost of supplies and rental truck and gasoline was about $5000. Dave, Wayne, and Nicki did almost all the work. I was the fetcher, payer, and deliverer.

The panels each had a decorative imprinting in the aluminum and they didn't all match. In fact, there were two different colors of panels. We're guys—we don't care. We also had many sheets of plywood, which were also affixed to the floor for stability, but the thing was watertight. I'd even bought windows that were imperfect and two doors, which we worked into the design. We ended up with two interior rooms with dividing walls of styro-aluminum and an 8x4 bathroom with a real toilet that flushes. Our running water consisted of the water we ran to get and ran back to a big tank that sometimes froze over. Our gas heater was a contribution I made when I found a nice one in a store in Florida. That heater could take the well-insulated cabin from freezing temperatures to warm and cozy in about 20 minutes. We installed a sink, fed by the water tank. Dave collected car batteries that still worked and charged them to give us 12 volt lights. Two queen-sized and a single bunk bed fit comfortably in the 16x16 bedroom, along with gun rack, chests, and clothes hooks. Two couches and a chair were found for the great room (also 16x16) and we were the proud creators and owners of a hunting cabin.

A log cabin could not be more snug. I anxiously look forward every year to spending that time with my "brothers" up there in that dwelling. There's never been a deep sleep like in that cabin. I've been told I snore, and Dave's wife says he's like a train, too...but we never hear each other, so our wives must be making that up. Food tastes great up there, cooking on the gas stove. Coming in from hunting wet and cold to a dry and warm camp is terrific. This is one of the only places where I can relax and let my stresses go out the window and into the woods. The hunting is very good, and I usually get about 4 days per year in the cabin and take home three deer. Alabama is generous with a buck and a doe each day limit for much of the season.

INSIGHT ONE: Why does a man invest $5000 in a cabin he only uses 4 to 5 days per year? That all depends upon how valuable those 4 to 5 days are to him, year after year. It's also important to me that even when I'm not there, Dave and his brothers can enjoy it. **We men are willing to invest in what we think is worthwhile.**

INSIGHT TWO: Everything that we do does not have to be for ourselves. It is an amazing thing to have the power within us to totally influence the joy or gloom of another person. We have a choice of which one to spread, joy or gloom? Too many choose the gloom of judgmentalism, negativism, and criticism. I want to invest positively in the lives of my family and of others, because I really believe that God put each of us here to make a huge difference in the world.

"What can one man do?" you ask. God has always worked through a minority of the people. One man with God's power can do a lot! I'm glad God allowed me to encourage and watch Dave, a Grizzly Adams look-alike (and nicknamed Griz), become a gentle giant among men. Dave is respected both for his many abilities (welding, mechanics, construction, managing people), for his strong work ethic, and for his love for God and his family. God let me be a little, tiny part of making that happen, and I feel honored and fulfilled. One regular person can be one majorly important part of God's blessing on someone else. Once in a while, I have that privilege.

Who do you have influence with? Is yours positive and encouraging, or abusive and negative? God gave you the power to change the lives of your wife, children, friends, neighbors, co-workers...to make 'em miserable or to make their life better. You say, "Nobody listens to me"? Well, that would tell me that you're using the power for negativity and they're choosing to ignore you. It's hard to ignore encouragement. What if you changed your tune and began to encourage, compliment, and thank people? Encouragement is powerful. In fact, if you're a boss or a dad or a husband, your instructive comments will be better received if you spend twice the time encouraging as correcting. Try it, dude. What can you lose? Nobody listens to you anyway.

INSIGHT THREE: Everyone doesn't have to be like you. My part in this adventure was to dream it, to acquire the pieces, to draw it up to share with my friends, to pay for it, and to deliver the parts to my friends. I helped little, because I lived too far. Their part was to build it, to put it together, but the best part came at the end of the road, as we now get to enjoy our cabin as a real comfortable and enjoyable part of every hunting trip.

Whatever you are doing, remember that others have different gifts than you do. Don't compare your best thing to their worst or your worst to their best. Different gifts don't make you competitors, they make you a complete team. That's true at work, at church, and at home. Freak your wife out today and tell her, "I'm glad we're different, because we're more of team because we have different gifts." Don't mess that up and say, "Boy, I sure am glad I'm not like you." That just won't work, pal, and it's better to say nothin' than to say it wrong.

1 Corinthians 12:12: The body is a unit, though it is made up of many parts;
and though all its parts are many, they form one body. So it is with Christ.

CHAPTER EIGHTEEN:
ANOTHER MISFIRE

I drove my truck across the dam at the Baumhower's and got out, loading my .270. I'd gotten a new box of shells but hadn't been to the gunsmith yet. The week before I had shot several times at a buck, but the shells hadn't gone off. I finally got him when a shell finally fired. I don't know why I thought the gun would just work this time, but I did!

I'm one of those guys who closes the truck door quietly, even if it's an hour or 30 minutes 'til daylight. You never know. So I loaded (are you allowed before daylight?) and took a step toward the woods road and heard twigs snap. It sounded like deer just ahead, but there were only a few stars out and the sun hadn't broken.

Now I had a decision to make. I can't stand here for 30 minutes 'til the sun comes up, when I might not see the deer anyway. It might not be a buck and I'd be standing for nothing. I knew that my stand for the day was a great one and I needed to be on it before daybreak when the deer came around the hill and up the gully.

I was curious about whether the deer in the woods in front of me was curious about me. My mind played with the fact that I had just gotten a six pointer last week and if I didn't get a deer today, it wouldn't matter that much. It was a simple question of a highly sophisticated brain and an animal brain, but I wasn't sure which one I had. I decided to stand there and wait. My eyes were adjusting to the darkness and I knew that the deer's eyes were already adjusted with his or her superior night vision. I thought again, "Isn't HE curious?" As I waited, the deer became a "he" in my mind, and this was indeed a battle of wits.

PHHhhhhh (I'm not certain how to spell this, but I think deer do more talking than reading anyway, so it doesn't matter if it's misspelled) came the snort from the trees just ahead, right beside the road. The sun peeked over the edge of the mountain and I could now see silhouettes of all the trees clearly. An eight-point buck stepped out of the trees and onto the road ten feet in front of me. It was a perfect broadside shot. I thought he might run (Yep, it was a HE alright.)

but pulled my gun to my shoulder. He stood. I was thankful that the shell was already in the chamber. (Yes, I had all of these thoughts in a blur of time. I told you I'm ADD and sometimes it just works to my advantage.) The scope was set for 3x and perfect as I looked at a picture perfect side silhouette of a deer, so clear that I could count the points. I squeezed the trigger and "click." Oh no! Not again! This deer could bolt at any time. What if the next shot doesn't fire? I'd better try. (Yep, all that thinkin' in an instant.) I did not try to be quiet. This time I was frustrated because I knew it wasn't the shells. There was something wrong with the gun itself.

Holding the scope on the deer, I slammed that shell out and another in and pulled (not squeezed) the trigger and BOOM. The deer groaned and dropped dead right there. All I had to do was turn my truck around because it was right behind me. I backed up to the deer and while I grabbed it to load, deer passed on both sides of me. They were everywhere. Bucks and does. Gun in car. Who cares? I got my eight point. I loaded him up and drove across the dam to the Baumhower house. Big Bob exclaimed, "Boy, he's pretty isn't he?" Yep, he was.

That's when I took my rifle to the gunsmith and showed him all the shells. He said it could only be one thing and confirmed that the firing pin was a hair too short. I got the gun fixed and had no further misfires.

INSIGHT ONE: It has been said that madness is doing the same thing over and over again in the same way while expecting different results. I thought I could solve the misfire problem by getting new shells, just like some of you might think you can solve your life problems by getting new friends, another job, a different church, a different wife, or moving to another location. The fact is that we can often fix a big part of the problem by some self investigation. It was the gun for me. This was a simple and inexpensive adjustment, but I could now expect success.

I meet guys in their third marriage wondering why they haven't found the perfect woman yet. If you found her, she wouldn't live with you. You're imperfect, too. That's the miracle! You take two imperfect people and make a relationship that is constantly improving because you're trying, or really sliding downhill because you're not. We constantly try to learn and improve our hunting skills to make us a better hunter and get more deer. Why wouldn't we try to become a better husband to have a better relationship with our wife and get more joy, more lovin', and more encouragement?

I meet guys that won't go to church because churches are imperfect places with imperfect people. Of course they are! You'd fit in perfectly because none of us has arrived. We're giving effort and becoming happier and liking ourselves more as we become a little more perfect every day, though we'll never arrive. Stop jumping from church to church, and start working to make your church better. Don't start with the preacher or members. Start with YOU doing ministry and make an effort in the areas where something needs to be done.

INSIGHT TWO: If you always got your deer every time you hit the woods and it was always better than your last deer, it would not be called hunting. It would be called "gettin'." The challenge would not be there if you scored every single time. If you missed the buck three times, but finally got 'im, what would that buck be worth? You would be an "overcomer."

In life, if you always succeeded, there would be no challenge. If you always scored, it wouldn't be sport. It is the challenge that makes it worthwhile. The Bible calls us MORE THAN CONQUERORS (Romans 8:35-37) even though we don't necessarily win every battle. Jesus actually admitted that (John 16:33) in this world we're going to have tough stuff to deal with, but that we shouldn't worry because He overcomes the world.

YOU CAN'T BE AN OVERCOMER
IF THERE'S NOTHING TO OVERCOME!

INSIGHT THREE: God knows we get frustrated sometimes. Don't you think He does? He's patient, but don't we push the limits? I love that the Bible acknowledges that we have it rough sometimes, then reminds us that when we follow Jesus, He fully intends success for us (Romans 12:21). It's a matter of overcoming our doubts and finding out that God means what He says (Mark 9:24).

Let's look at Mr. Smartbuck. Your buddies swear they saw this buck stop and read the sign that says NO HUNTING, then went and stood behind that sign smiling! Now, that's a smart buck. He's outsmarted most of your friends and lived through at least four seasons. He even outsmarted you when he sneaked by in a gully with only his antlers showing. But this year is different. This year you took a different position and could see into that gully and sure enough, there he comes sneaking down the gully. At the last minute, he turns, jumps out among some pine trees, and runs right past the stand you sat in last year. Now, what buck would you rather "overcome" more than any other buck in the woods? That's called the challenge, the sport of hunting.

So now, in life you're trying to overcome a problem, and you've failed time after time. This last time you learned something about yourself and about the problem, and you have a whole new way of looking at it. Now you know you can whoop it because it is no longer the central concentration of your life. You are now bigger than the problem. Maybe it's the boss at work. He's targeting you and finds something wrong with everything you do. He gives you the dirty jobs and the ones that are impossible. He approaches you again and tells you that you did the job sloppily, and instead of your usual angry facial expression , instead of arguing with him, instead of excuses, you say, "Well, let me clock out here and do it right on my own time, Mr. Smith. Can you show me what else you want done?" Now, the guy may still be picky and nasty, but he doesn't get to you and he can see that. You're no longer mad at him because you're bigger than him. Yes, you are under control and because of that YOU are in control of how you respond and you are bigger than him. He's the boss, even if he's wrong and he's trying to dominate your anger and emotions, but he is no longer in control. You are officially an overcomer.

John 16:33: I have told you these things, so that in me you may have peace.
In this world you will have trouble. But take heart! I have overcome the world. (Jesus)

CHAPTER NINETEEN:
THE NO-PLACE-TO-HUNT GEORGIA BUCK

A Hunting Lease is a great thing if you're in on the leasing. Most of the places I used to hunt are now unavailable, except to the club that leases it. One year I was totally left out-in-the-cold. I had no place to hunt in Florida, where I lived, or in Alabama, where I loved to return and hunt with my buddy Dave.

Dale and Barbara, some of my church members, found out about my dilemma and invited me to their summer home in Georgia, saying he'd find some neighbors who would let me hunt. I'd never hunted in Georgia and this sounded pretty good, so I headed up that way. Wow, they had a nice place for me to stay, and they fed me! What a deal! Dale and Barbara McAllister were just wonderful hosts. They let me bring along my friend Al, as well. This was Al's second hunt.

We drove over to the neighbor's place, about 10 miles away, and he walked us through the land the evening before. I would be near a creek bottom, and I marked the unused trail to my deer stand with reflective tape. Little did I know that the man's son would find that tape when he came out from his stand that night and remove all of it.

In the darkness of a morning with no stars shining, I was dropped off and headed into the woods. I began by walking down a road just inside the woods-line and past an old lifeguard chair that someone had put there as a deer stand. No camo, just a point of view with a ladder seat. I walked by and to the creek bottom to cross and pick up my reflective trail. It was not there. My heart was filled with anticipation and the bottom just dropped out right there. I thought I'd try to find that deer stand myself, so in I went, listening to the creek and moving toward the place where I thought the stand was. I never could find it. In addition to that problem, I was a bit lost, which is unusual for me. My inborn GPS was not getting a signal, so I went to the creek to follow it down. Little did I know there were several splits in that creek and I was following a different branch than I thought. I came out at a road, about forty yards from the place where the car had dropped me off.

All that anticipation was gone, leaving a hole in my heart the size of the Grand Canyon. I had no hope of success. I'd even dreamed of that unfound deer stand the night before. It was broad daylight now. I walked down the little road and climbed into the lifeguard chair. The creek ran down below, but the undergrowth was so high that you couldn't see to the creek. At one place in the bottom, there was high grass that reached about five feet. Suddenly, the woods were alive with crashing, and the high grass was alive with tails bounding everywhere, but I couldn't see. I suspected dogs chasing the deer, but there was no barking and no dogs came through. Then I realized that this was the height of the rut and it was probably a buck chasing does...and here I was...Mr. Lifeguard. I wondered if those deer had run under the stand I was supposed to be in. I was emotionally bottomed out. How could things get worse?

I had to pee. Oh, yeah, things can get worse. Why did I even ask the question? I reached into my camo backpack and pulled out the pee bottle. It was that year's model apple juice bottle with a wide-mouth to make me feel manly. I hung my rifle, Dad's .270 Remington Pump, on a tree branch by the sling, stood up in the lifeguard chair, undid the pants, and began to find relief when I looked down in the woods. In the shadows was one of the stumps, shaped just like a deer. The stump had an eight-point rack and was standing broadside, while I was standing up in a lifeguard chair, peeing in a bottle with my pants open and my rifle hanging on a branch. I did not feel like more-than-a-conqueror or an overcomer.

Please understand that even though this sounds like a long process, the following happened very quickly. First, I had to put down the pee bottle on the arm of the lifeguard chair, while holding my pants up. Next I fastened the button on my pants and didn't bother with the zipper. (That could happen later.) Now I reached for the .270, pulled it up while standing in the chair, sighted in the buck (that's no stump, buddy) and squeezed off. The buck simply slumped to the ground. My first Georgia deer was on the ground. I zipped, belted, put the cap on the bottle, put the bottle in the backpack, climbed down the little ladder, and made my way to the deer.

Neighbors told me it was the biggest deer ever taken in that area. I really didn't care! It was a deer, and I was not "skunked" by the lost stand or by getting lost. I would never have chosen that spot to hunt and still would not choose it. (Well, maybe I would.) If I'd followed my original plan for the day, I may not have succeeded. What began as a day with hopes demolished became quite a nice day.

INSIGHT ONE: Defeat comes only when we give up. Winston Churchill said it, "Never, never, never give up." On the day described in this story, I did...almost. I'm so glad I didn't pack it up and go to the

The No-Place-to-Hunt Georgia Buck

house. Instead, I sat (and stood, and grumbled) in an unlikely stand and bagged an unlikely buck. Some of us predict our own defeat at work, at marriage, as a dad, as a hunter by quitting just before victory time. Endurance counts! You might be able to add a list of your own to my list of frustrations, and it sure feels good when I can proceed and succeed in spite of the frustrations. Life can really stink sometimes, but you never know when some opportunity may come up. Be ready for it. Never give up! Never, never, never...

INSIGHT TWO: If you read the story, you'll realize the ups and downs of my emotions.

> **Down** – no place to hunt.
> **Up** – found a place to hunt with good friends, good food, good hunting country, and a good stand.
> **Down** – someone removed my reflective tape, I can't find my stand, I'm lost, I followed the wrong stream, it's daylight and I don't want to tromp the woods and spoil my chances or the chances of others.
> **Up** – I can hunt from this lifeguard chair.
> **Down** – I don't want to hunt from the lifeguard chair, I can't see the stream, I can't make out the deer running around, I have to pee.
> **Up** – there's an eight-point buck.
> **Down** – my pants are partly-open, my hand is filled with the pee bottle, my gun is hanging on the tree, I have to squat down to put down the bottle, fasten my pants, and pick up the gun. (I guess I could have shot 'im with my pants down. That would make a good story.)
> **Up** – I have the gun, he's in the scope, he's down, and I got the best buck in the county for some years.

Don't ride the attitude roller coaster. My attitude did not affect that buck coming on site for my shot. Only if I'd given up and left, or ceased to look for deer, would I have failed. In spite of my attitude, I did not quit. Guys, don't quit. **Whatever it is that's dragging you down, don't quit. Never, never, never...**

Philippians 4:8: Finally, brothers, whatever is true, whatever is noble, whatever is right,
whatever is pure, whatever is lovely, whatever is admirable—
if anything is excellent or praiseworthy—think about such things.
9 Whatever you have learned or received or heard from me,
or seen in me—put it into practice. And the God of peace will be with you.

CHAPTER TWENTY:
AN ARROW ESCAPE

I'm very good with a rifle. No brag, just fact. I have a lot of experience, and I've taken my share of deer, even when no one else was getting any. I've made shots that amazed myself. As I heard others talk about bow hunting, I became more and more curious. The challenge seemed to be greater than rifle hunting, and I met several guys who had totally gone to bow hunting, even in rifle season.

Of course, I didn't have a bow and they were quite expensive. Richard Kiser is one of my hunting buddies for wild hog and deer in recent years. He's the International Country Gospel Music Association's Musician of the Decade and a tremendous guitarist. I've had the opportunity to play guitar behind Richard and behind Charlie McCoy on his harmonica. Well, I had the privilege of taking Richard out for his first successful wild boar hunt, and several more hunts after that, with his pistol, his black powder rifle, and his bow. Richard had a new bow and would sell me the old bow, case, and arrows and a Roland guitar synthesizer adapter that I wanted for $150. I took it and began to practice. I needed a backstop behind the target as practice arrows skimmed off the ground and toward my neighbor's house, once just missing his screen around the pool. Finally, I felt I was ready...if the deer stood perfectly still at a distance of about 15 yards, broadside, and was willing to jump to where the arrow was going and take the hit, I could possibly score.

I ventured out twice that year. The first time I missed a big doe at about 30 yards as I shot right under her chest into the ground behind her. While I was still telling God He should have sent that deer another 10 yards closer, a big boar hog came crashing through the woods behind me and came out on the dirt road in front of my stand. I "arrowed-up" (I don't know the real name for putting the arrow on the thingy and snapping the doo-dad onto the string). I snapped my "doo-dad" on the string and drew back as the big ol' fella trotted away and I let fly. He squealed (not with glee) as I nicked his manly (piggly?) parts and the arrow stuck into the ground between where his legs had been. He jumped, turned up the speed, and scampered into the woods. Wow! Two misses in one day—a doe and a boar.

I went home and practiced some more, but not enough. The next Saturday I was on that same stand when a doe came down the road and stopped at 10 yards in front of me. I could almost hear God saying, "Try that distance, Rick," as He and the angels lined up at cloud's edge to watch. I drew back and the arrow fell off the whatchamacallit and clanged against the bow. The deer took off and stopped right under me. I didn't know how to make a shot like that. (I didn't know how to make ANY shot.) I drew back and shot straight down into the dirt and the deer trotted back to where it started from. This deer was mocking me, guys. It looked like about 15 yards this time and I wasn't going to shoot under this deer like the last deer and boar. *Thoook*, the arrow sailed right over her back, perfectly aligned with the chest but just a bit high. The deer walked under a big branch and I never saw her again. (I thought I heard her chuckle, though—either she or those angels who were watching from the cloud.)

I skipped the next year of bow hunting. A guy can only take so much humiliation. This year, though, I'm practicing. I've shot 'til my shoulders ached...both of them. They've never been this weak, but they are getting stronger. Every arrow goes into the target and many of them to the bullseye. Thirty five yards is my next goal, as well as working on the ability to know which sight to choose at what distance. You won't have to read it in a book or an email when I get my first deer or hog with a bow. You'll hear me yelling three states away!

INSIGHT ONE: No matter how good you are at some things, there are other things you won't be as good at. There's always more to learn. Remembering this, we should never put the other guy down because he can't do what we can do. He may be good at something else that we aren't gifted in. So respect each person for what he does and don't judge him by your greatest skill area. Now reverse that! Don't put yourself down because you don't do everything well. Realize what you're good at and thank God that we're all different and we need each other to be really equipped for life.

INSIGHT TWO: Preparation is a key to success. I was not prepared enough to be out on a hunt. I hear people gripe all the time that opportunity has never knocked at their door except when they weren't home. You were home! You just weren't prepared. I'm thinking of asking my wife to bake cookies for the Publisher's Clearing House Prize Patrol this year, just in case they come. Being "ready" is very important. Being "prepared" means practice, study, and taking the goal seriously enough to put the time in.

INSIGHT THREE: Just because I failed (three shots worth on one deer) **doesn't make me a failure.** Everyone strikes out occasionally, and so will you. **You are not a failure until you stop trying.** Other opportunities will come. We just have to accept that this failure at hand is not a life sentence. I can learn from this. Someone said, "I have learned more from my failures than from my successes." If I knew who he was, I'd give him credit.

Remember when your child took his first step, then tumbled to the floor, breaking his fall with his nose? Did you yell, "Stupid kid, you fell!" or did you yell, "Wow! Your first step. You're growing up." Didn't you pick him up and encourage him to try again? "Now, walk to Daddy." Well, when God looks down at our stupid mistakes that come from trying to do better, He does not yell, "Stupid man, you blew it!" He says, "I created you on purpose and it is My will for you succeed. What did you learn from this time that will help you next time to avoid that mistake? Are you ready? I'll go with you. Let's try again, little buddy!" What's that you say? You're not little? Well, you are when compared to God who looks on you like his son.

1 Corinthians 12:14: Now the body is not made up of one part but of many. 15 If the foot should say, "Because I am not a hand, I do not belong to the body," it would not for that reason cease to be part of the body. 16 And if the ear should say, "Because I am not an eye, I do not belong to the body," it would not for that reason cease to be part of the body. 17 If the whole body were an eye, where would the sense of hearing be? If the whole body were an ear, where would the sense of smell be? 18 But in fact God has arranged the parts in the body, every one of them, just as he wanted them to be. 19 If they were all one part, where would the body be? 20 As it is, there are many parts, but one body. 21 The eye cannot say to the hand, "I don't need you!" And the head cannot say to the feet, "I don't need you!" 22 On the contrary, those parts of the body that seem to be weaker are indispensable, 23 and the parts that we think are less honorable we treat with special honor. And the parts that are unpresentable are treated with special modesty, 24 while our presentable parts need no special treatment. But God has combined the members of the body and has given greater honor to the parts that lacked it...

CHAPTER TWENTY-ONE:
FREEZER BURNED?

I lost three deer and a hog in our church freezer when it failed. They thawed, and I grieved. I didn't really cry, but I was really disappointed that I got "burned" by that freezer (freezer burn?). I'd had a good year and I wanted to have a big wild game cookout for the church.

The first wild game cookout only succeeded because we promised regular tame pork, as well as the wild boar, venison, and other specialties. Funny thing is that some of the very "proper" folks decided to just take one taste of the wild venison and pork to say they'd tried it. At the end of the banquet there was lots of beef and pork loin left, but the wild meat was gone. We converted 'em.

There are two of us out of four at my house who will eat venison. I'm a lover of smoking meats. I don't mean an hour on the barbecue gas grill, boys. I mean in the smoker with oak and hickory in the fire box, build the fire up then bring it down and put the meat in for overnight...maybe 12 hours. Boy, that's some eatin'. Problem is that I get smoked, too. My nostrils get so smoked I have to clean 'em out with my wife's toothbrush when she's not looking. I breathe woodsmoke and swallow it so much that I make hickory flavored bathroom stops for the next several days. But I still do it, because I love to see the look on my friends faces when they say, "Mmmm, this Bro's Barbecue is the best I've ever had."

Bro? Oh, I told you before that "Bro" is my nickname. It's short for Brother, because as a pastor I don't like to be called reverend. As you read in the previous paragraph about the bathroom stops, I'm not always that reverent. So from now on, you can call me "Bro," "PR," Pastor Rick, or just Rick.

Smoking meats is an art. Some do it like crayons and paper, and others do it like Picasso. You don't want the meat to get dry, but you want it permeated with that smoky taste. I use venison, wild hog, beef roasts, and pork loins mostly. I sure hate I lost those 3 deer and the hog.

Some like to eat that smoked meat without sauce, but my sauce is special. The base is Cattlemen's Smokey Sauce, but I do things to it that will make your taste buds double in size. If you set a piece of sauce-soaked, smoked Bro's barbecued meat on top of your head, your tongue will beat your brains out trying to get to it. What's in it? Well, I already told you about the Cattlemen's and there's brown sugar, vinegar, and several other secret ingredients. Have me over to eat sometime and I'll bring the sauce.

INSIGHT ONE: Why do things like this decimate us? I mean, I lost three deer and a pig. It's a shame and no one's fault. We'd have to have a banquet with regular food, but we can do that. The earth hasn't stopped and life goes on. I begin to wonder how much of my life I've wasted feeling sorry for myself and mourning something that can't be changed. Just take a look and decide what CAN be done. Each thing is a battle, but the campaign goes on. **Let's make a promise to each other that we will spend less time crying over our losses and get back into the game sooner.**

INSIGHT TWO: Smoking meats brings me pleasure, but others think it's pretty dumb. They'd just as soon buy some ribs from the roadside guy with the trailer cooker...and his are pretty good. They think I'm using a lot of time doing something that doesn't matter. It matters to me. If something gives you pleasure and it's not sin or wrong or selfish, you go for it, brother. If it's not taking valuable time or money away from your family or keeping you from worship on Sunday, or hurting your body, dive in. Those who would say it's a waste of time are just wasting their time doing other things. **Many people don't know how to enjoy anything in life, and you are way ahead of them.**

INSIGHT THREE: When smoking meats smokes me, it's miserable. **There are some things in life that have a cost, and we have to figure whether or not it is worth the cost.** So figure it out. Is it? If not, invest yourself in something more worthwhile. I keep smoking meats because I like to share the end result with my friends. They don't have to know all the ins and outs, the pains and pleasures. They just taste and smile. I love those smiles.

Philippians 3:13: ...Forgetting what is behind and straining toward what is ahead, 14 I press on
toward the goal to win the prize for which God has called me heavenward in Christ Jesus.

CHAPTER TWENTY-TWO:
AN A.D.D. HUNTER

Having A.D.D. can be exciting or painful. If you have it, your entire life is affected in every way. A.D.D. affects my hunting, working, thinking, loving, planning, public speaking, and my entire life. I can't sit on a porch doing nothing, but I can sit on a deer stand for hours without moving, just watching the area around me. In that time, I sit and listen for God and tune in to the beauty so that I won't miss a thing.

As a child I struggled with the **creative chaos** that ran rampant in my mind as I imagined stories, listened to the teacher, and thought about what I'd do after school. When you get all that wild-horse creativity into one harness, pulling the same direction, it's great.

You parents whose children have A.D.D. may have spent nights in tears, worrying about what will become of him or her. Spend time in prayer, do your best, and watch for great results. Many of these kids are hyper and intelligent, though socially explosive. They can learn facts, and they can learn behavior. They can learn to train that mind to work for them and not just to have that mind dominate them into chaotic activity. Be thankful for the creativity while you help them to learn to focus.

I was never bored growing up. No matter what I was doing, I was doing six or seven different things at the same time. My mind kept track of all those lines of thinking, but I wasn't always tuned in with my eyes on the teacher. I got ridiculed by some teachers and nurtured by others. None of them ruined me. My mother, my grandfather, and my Pastor worked with me. I began to preach when they asked for volunteers from the church youth group. I was in 7th grade. I sang in the choir at age 10 and could sing the tenor part because I could hear it. It drove my brothers crazy as I went around the house singing the tenor part, and they cried out, "That's not how the song goes."

That's another point. I was in another dimension in my way of thinking, and they were in theirs. Both of my brothers excelled at music and actually were trained to read and write music. I never read or wrote music, because I never needed to. I heard the three people ahead of me sing a part to audition for state chorus, and I simply memorized it and sang by memory when it was my turn, pretending to look at the song sheet. I made it! If I heard a song sung by a quartet, I could learn all four parts and memorize them in one listening.

In the woods, there is much going on in my mind, but I've learned to tune-out what I don't want to think about and tune in to my surroundings and to my God. I listen. I watch and learn. If you have an A.D.D. child, I ask you to let him or her read this and take hope. My sermons are better because I'm able to "shift gears" and demonstrate the scriptures through the stories that God places in my mind to illustrate them. So thank God for the way you are (or your child is) and then set out to "tune yourself" (him or her) to succeed at your God-given dreams.

INSIGHT ONE: Many parents are destroyed by the idea that their child is A.D.D. **Rejoice that your child has a healthy body and a teachable mind. Start right where you are and realize that the changes will come over time and not all at once.** Celebrate the little victories along the way.

INSIGHT TWO: Many of you may have used your A.D.D. as an excuse. It is not a curse and you are not a victim. Other people deal with other problems. **Use your "problem" to your advantage.** That creativity is a blessing. You are a party of joy, looking for a place to happen. Start right now. The rest of your life starts from right here. Look at yourself. Look to God and go forward into a wonderful plan for your life.

INSIGHT THREE: Many people will not understand you if you have this trait. It is more important that you understand yourself. Why am I like this? Because this is my starting point. I can change what I want, but I want to keep some of this energy and enthusiasm as I decide what to get rid of. Pray for the ones who don't understand you. **You are not required to think like everyone else.**

1 Corinthians 10:31: So whether you eat or drink or whatever you do, do it all for the glory of God.

CHAPTER TWENTY-THREE:
WOULD THE REAL TURKEY PLEASE STAND UP?

My step dad, my step brother, and I walked up the logging road. We'd driven in the jeep as far as we could drive, but the road was too muddy and soft. Fall turkey season in Pennsylvania is a rifle hunt, sometimes shooting from mountain to mountain. We stopped at the head of a hollow and I got my instructions. I was to find a place to sit hidden, and the two of them would walk out the ridge and come back this way down either side of the hollow. They left. The first thing I noticed was the hollow stump with one side broken out. It made a perfect seat and only my feet and my head showed. It was comfortable. I leaned back and could see in all directions and it was comfortable. I had no silhouette and the entire hollow was visible and ...it ... was ...comfortable...zzzz.

When I awakened there was a big ol' splotchy red face right next to mine. If you're familiar with that and you're thinking of your wife, you might want to keep it to yourself, husbands. No, I'm talking about wild turkey all around me. I was in the middle of a flock, asleep. I didn't want to move too quickly, but I'd leaned my rifle beside me. I'd never done a turkey impression and I figured they wouldn't be fooled anyway. I grabbed my rifle and the flock exploded in every direction as the rest of my party came on the scene. Oh, what ridicule I took. Oh, I deserved it, too.

Not one of us bagged a turkey that day or that year. In fact, I have still never killed a turkey. I've never been spring gobbler hunting. I'm ready for Spring Gobbler season, but there's that problem with permission to hunt and no land lease. All the land is leased down here in Florida, and the Osceola turkey is a major prize that northern hunters pay guides big money to hunt. Maybe someday, but I can't say I didn't have my chance on that day in the tree stump.

INSIGHT ONE: When you don't pay attention, you may find yourself surrounded by turkeys. Suddenly you realize it and don't know how it happened, but your friends are all drunk, disorderly, foul-mouthed, drug-addicted, disrespectful to their wives, and ugly, and you're doing a pretty good turkey impression yourself. Be aware, guys, that you can't soar with the eagles when you're surrounded by turkeys. Birds of a feather...you know the rest. Choose the folks you want to be around. Either find folks who are like you'd like to be...or do like Jesus did: hang out with the drunks and thieves in order to help them find their way to eagle-dom. Don't let them lead you. We're not better than each other, but we're all here to help each other be better.

INSIGHT TWO: When life gets comfortable, rest but don't get careless. I let the team down on that turkey hunt. There's still work to be done, and other people are counting upon you. You're part of a team in your family, your workplace, your church. Don't be the one who lets others down. Whether you are the star-up-front or the strength in the background, don't get lazy about your role in this world. Your part is too important, whether you realize it or not.

1 Corinthians 15:33: Do not be misled:
"Bad company corrupts good character."

CHAPTER TWENTY-FOUR:
THE LEGEND OF THE BLIND BUCK

I thought it was a legend, but there he was. It wasn't that the buck was so big; he had nine points on a decent rack. The legend was that a doe had kept her blind fawn alive by having him follow her by holding her tail in his mouth. Various stories told how that the young buck was forced away by courting bucks for the first two years and that she would return to him afterward to lead him with her tail. It sounded hokey to me. I had stopped laughing at the stories, because they insulted my intelligence (at least what intelligence remains in a guy 50+ who still climbs twenty feet into the trees to get a deer).

It was a clear morning after a rainy night. I chose a ladder stand about a quarter mile downhill from the cabin and in the swamp. Still a bit sleepy, I leaned back against the tree with my waterproof jacket. I was fighting falling asleep in the early darkness. There would be no telltale noises to let me know something was coming, as the ground was so wet. The sun was now peeking through the trees. A coyote moved through the trees like a ghost floating above the ground. I watched him as he glided through the woods.

On the hillside is a movement and I can see several doe moving quietly toward me. I can take a doe or a buck, but it is a hard drag through the swamp and up the hill, so I'll likely let the doe go by. Something caught the rising sun, however. It was a glint of a beam of the antlers of the last deer. I look through my scope and grow numb in disbelief. A nine-point buck is following the doe. At first it seems he is sniffing, perhaps getting the scent of the doe being in heat. That's not the case. That buck has the doe's tail in his mouth. I can't believe my eyes.

Two questions hit me. The first is whether I want to end a legend. The guys will never believe what I am seeing, whether I shoot him or not. Then again, a nine-point buck is hard to pass on, regardless of the long and arduous drag ahead.

The creative wheels begin to turn, and I suddenly realized that I could prove the legend and save the long, uphill drag at the same time. I take careful aim near the base of the doe's tail and whistle softly. The doe stops, as does the buck. This will need to be a precise shot. I squeeze carefully on the trigger. The doe runs at the sound of the shot, leaving her tail behind in the mouth of the buck...the perfect shot. He, in turn, doesn't know where to run. He is blind. The tail is not pulling him in any direction. He walks ahead, tail in mouth, and runs into a tree.

I reach into my backpack and pull out doe-in-estrus scent to overpower my human scent. I smear it on my pants and then it's time to approach the buck. I take hold of the tail. He is sniffing noticeably, as he smells the doe scent and realizes, "This is not my mom." With the tail, I begin to lead him though the swamp and up the hill. I'll lead him right to camp and shoot him there. He occasionally tries to get closer and I wish I hadn't done the doe scent thing. I am not giving him a ride up the hill, no matter how much I want to avoid this drag! In the meantime, I may have put on too much scent, because two other smaller bucks are following at a distance. I'm getting a little nervous here.

When the guys see me coming they rise slowly from their seats around the picnic table outside the cabin. Their jaws are dropping as I come into sight with a big buck behind me and two smaller ones trailing. They don't know whether to go for their guns, their cameras, or what. I motion toward the tail in my hand, and they realize that this is the famous blind buck. As I close in, one of the men throws a rope around the nine point's neck and the other little bucks run off. One of the guys grabs my pant leg and begins to pull. The others join into a practice I've never seen in any hunting club. They are pulling and pulling my leg, just like I've been pulling yours through this entire story.

INSIGHT ONE: Did you want to quit reading when you realized I was pulling your leg? Did you keep going? Some of us just can't quit once we've begun, but we need to. **It's easier to continue going in a wrong direction than changing, but wrong directions don't take us to our goal.** Sometimes we need to adjust our direction. For some of us that may mean changing college majors, changing jobs, or changing habits (especially those that are destroying our relationships and success). We adjust and fine-tune our scopes, but we don't do anything about our lives. We carefully plan our hunts, but just allow real life to happen to us as though we had no choice. Why not plan for life? I know sometimes plans don't work, but don't we still make plans for each hunt? Doesn't wise planning increase our chance of success? Will you continue the same patterns of life or adjust your direction? Changing is tough, but not changing costs too much. Realize whether the path you are on will lead you to where you want to go. If the answer is "Yes," congratulations! If it's "No," it might be time to change direction.

INSIGHT TWO: Imagination is fun. Really, I love the dreams I used to have of flying through the air. Luckily, I didn't try 'em out from a rooftop. Every hunter dreams, and the feeling of fulfillment is just as consuming as reality, except when you wake up. Why? Why not smile at the dream and move out to make it reality? I have friends who have had great hunts in reality and were disappointed because they figured they had now experienced the best they would ever find and the thrill of future hunting was over. It doesn't take an ultimate trophy to make the best hunt. Just the challenge of each hunt makes it an adventure.

What if we faced each day with the same theory? You may think your glory days are behind you, as you were a high school football hero (in our own mind...I mean we didn't go pro, did we?) or great rock musician (but those days are over without making millions on national tours). Our long hair may now be a very smooth head. Our major bodybuilding days have been replaced by the exercise of just trying to get out of bed in the morning. So what? Each day has its own challenge. Back then, we tried to impress others to build our self-esteem. By now, we've learned the gift of knowing our own value in our own eyes and within our own system of values. Our challenge goals will be based upon what we have to work with. It's not a matter of lowering the bar. It's a matter of being realistic. Otherwise we will face the frustration of approaching unreachable goals and constantly failing. Challenging goals are acceptable, but we each compete (with ourselves) in our own category. Remember wrestling? You were in weight classes. Remember high school football? They didn't let you play anymore after you graduated. Same with college sports. So don't stop challenging yourself, but do it within the range of you own weight and age class. There are still challenges worth pursuing.

Genesis 1:1: In the beginning, God created...

CHAPTER TWENTY-FIVE:
MY BEST BUCK SO FAR

Remember the apple tree I spoke of many chapters ago, the one where my gun kept misfiring? Well, that is one special hunting spot. I've seen and taken many deer from that stand. I've sat in that tree in the mornings before light and in the evenings until darkness. It is just a flat platform you can sit on at the top of a wooden ladder. There is a special branch, however, that you can lean up against while you sit, that makes it feel like a La-Z-Boy recliner. Well, I spent hours in that tree.

One evening, I sat in that stand 'til the sun began to set. There was no frustration about not seeing a buck to shoot. I just love being outdoors. It is the hunting that thrills me, not just the getting. The quiet and the breeze, a passing coyote or even a raccoon brings a smile to my face. And then it's getting dusk and time to call it a night.

I turned my back to find the first step down the ladder and something stopped me. Slowly, I turned and looked in the failing light. There on the edge of the grass field was a big buck with its head down eating.

He may have been bedded in the five-foot-high weeds that bordered the planted field. I wasn't too concerned with where he used to be. It was just exciting to have him here and now. I stepped back up and turned my bottom around on the stand to take hold of my rifle. This was a nice buck and I could see the rack with my bare eyeballs. I would not shoot if I didn't have a good shot and enough light. The buck was very visible in the scope and the crosshairs were clear. I squeezed that trigger and could see the flash of the muzzle. He turned and crashed into the high weeds.

I walked to where he had stood and found good blood. Still, I was hesitant to enter that high grass alone. It was the heat of the rut and if that wounded buck injured me, no one would know where I was. I always felt it was important that they would find my body if I was skewered by an antler out in the wild.

Dave drove over when he heard the shot. We began to drive his truck through the five-foot weeds with his headlights on. I stood in the bed with a flashlight. That guy would drive that truck anywhere, like it was four-wheel-drive, and I don't ever remember getting stuck. On our second pass of the field, I suddenly saw the flash of white underbelly and there was the deer.

It's amazing that a deer that looks so big when you shoot can shrink by the time you reach that big boy. Sometimes you think "this must be another deer." Not this time, boys. This buck was bigger than it looked in the dusk through the scope. I'm not the kind of guy who dances... but I did. I danced all around that deer. Eight points, nice brow tines, and a good sized body. Oh, he wasn't Boone and Crockett, but he was the best I'd ever shot to that day.

Now, some of you may scold me for shooting at dusk, but I promise that if you had seen this deer standing still at 50 yards, clear in the scope with the crosshairs fixed, antlers shining, your finger would have sneaked its way to the trigger for a pull.

INSIGHT ONE: The hunt isn't over until the very end of that day. You can go without seeing a deer all day, only to see the monster in the last moment. There is no such thing as a "time-out" during the hunt. I've seen some really good deer when we stopped being quiet and were joking and laughing while eating candy bars. I've drifted off to a snooze, only to wake up to see deer disappear over the ridge, having walked by. Oh, I know that most of you would never tell that on yourself, but fact is fact. Every minute of a hunt is valuable.

INSIGHT TWO: I don't mind hunting alone, but someone should know where I am. If you are hurt, they need to know where to search. Hunters get hurt by falling out of their tree stand when not wearing a harness, and though I've never fallen, I have resisted the intelligence of wearing such a harness. I have stepped on a slippery rock and slid, twisting my ankle. I know of other hunters who have broken a leg in the woods. Heart attacks? They can happen when we've been in the recliner too long and thought we could still drag a deer for ½ mile. Let someone know where you are.

My sons never appreciated my asking where they would be when they left the house. They were a little defensive in that area. Still, I tell my wife where I am going just as a matter of consideration, and if I am late, I call to let her know. If my boys go into downtown Tampa to do a concert, I want to know where to look if something goes wrong. So no apologies to them or to you...let someone know where you'll be.

INSIGHT THREE: One of the enjoyments of hunting is reliving the experience. It's fun to hear the stories of others and share your own. It's a chance to do it over again without the cold weather or effort. So each hunt is good for dozens of reruns!

INSIGHT FOUR: Why do I say, "my best buck so far"? Well, I wouldn't mind getting a better one. **I never want to stop anticipating new accomplishments. They can happen at any time.** This deer hangs on the guest room wall, looking down at our friends as they sleep. I've wanted to put red light bulbs behind the eyes and terrorize a few folks, but have resisted the urge for fear of heart attacks and lawsuits. If I get a bigger one, though, I'll let you know!

Colossians 4:5: Be wise in the way you act toward outsiders; make the most of every opportunity.

CHAPTER TWENTY SIX:
THE BEST BUCKS I'VE EVER SEEN #1

Behind the Baumhower's Plantation was another property owned by a guy named Steve. Steve was a mega-millionaire from the oil industry and had a phenomenal amount of beautiful land, covered with oaks, nice fields, and loaded with deer. Once in a while he would invite the Baumhowers to come back and hunt. There were phenomenal deer there near Demopolis, Alabama. On one trip, Steve required shotguns, and I didn't have one with me. All I had at that time was the .32 special and my .270. He said, "Take the .32 Special." So I did what he said.

At the beginning of the hunt we were told to shoot only doe and messed-up cull bucks (bucks with poor racks) that he wouldn't want to reproduce. This would be a drive and there would be about 10 of us. As we rode the back of a pickup toward where we would hunt, five bucks broke across the field in front of us. All of us were aghast. Each buck carried from 12 to 18 points and Steve took the opportunity to remind us that those weren't the deer we were after.

I was dropped off in a field near there and told to go to the woods edge to wait for the deer driven through. As I waited, I heard shotguns firing the entire time. There were too many doe on the property and they needed thinned. This sounded like a really good thinning because the shotguns sounded like the 4th of July back there. Suddenly a deer was running toward me through the thick trees, a puny, scraggly spike buck that needed taken out of the gene pool. The trees were really thick, but he saw me and went running to the right. I couldn't get a shot.

As I turned back, the boy's club was entering the field. There was the "gang" we had seen earlier, about 30 yards away and prancing around broadside. They were trophies-of-a-lifetime and I wasn't allowed to fire. I put the iron sights on 'em just to get the feel. It felt terrible because I wasn't allowed to shoot. I have never had such an opportunity, but it seemed the deer knew I couldn't shoot. They just kept prancing around. The word prancing really fits what they were doing. It was like they were showing off.

I knew if I shot, I'd never be allowed on the property again. I also knew that my reputation and integrity were on trial here. I did not shoot.

Soon afterward the men began to emerge from the woods and the deer melted into a little creek bed that seemed too small to hold or hide them. There they laid down and just disappeared. Out of all of that shooting there had only been three doe killed. I am still haunted by the vision of those bucks playing together out in the field so close to where I stood. It seems too perfect to see such awesome animals in that setting, but I was there and it makes me so grateful for the opportunity.

INSIGHT ONE: Guys, there are things in life that we can appreciate from afar, but shouldn't buy. It could be a Porsche, too big a house, or a woman that is not and should not be yours. Appreciate the beauty, but don't covet or lust. Appreciate the great things God gave you. If you see something beautiful that is not to be yours, just say, "Good job, God," and then get your eyes away before lust sets in.

INSIGHT TWO: I wonder how those deer knew they were not in danger from me? Had they seen me miss before? For some reason they weren't worried about me. I could have been a real danger, but they just weren't afraid. They were right! I wasn't allowed to shoot them.

How many times in life have we worried about what might happen...that never happened? We suffered anxiety, headache, gastro problems, and fatigue about something that never came to be. We suffered as though it really happened. Maybe we even became irritable with our family members over something that would never come to be true. Worry doesn't benefit us. Awareness does and preparedness does, but this thing of worry is a waste of time, life, and joy. What are you worried about? Is it possible that it may not happen? Are you going to suffer anyway?

Philippians 4:6 NLT: Don't worry about anything;
instead, pray about everything.
Tell God what you need, and thank him for all he has done.

CHAPTER TWENTY-SEVEN:
THE BEST BUCK I'VE EVER SEEN #2

I'd had a great nap that afternoon. A warm hunting cabin can feel so good in the afternoon on a cold day. I felt great in the shooting house that evening. Several doe had come into the field and were content to feed, unaware of my presence. I meant them no harm, but I was waiting for their boyfriend. They were legal to take, but I wanted a buck.

I love to just watch the deer browse lazily as the younger ones trot around the field. This was a special night, as perhaps ten of them wandered around. Dusk began to settle in, and a large doe joined the others. I was losing light. The field was very visible, but the deer in the woods were now invisible to my eyes. Now the dusk was settling in the field, but some movement caught my eye. From the far end where the swamp began, a huge deer was approaching with head down. Even in the low light I could see the gleam of those antlers, wide beyond the body. He approached the biggest doe and stood broadside in front of her. Although dim, I could see the silhouette perfectly in my scope and if the bullet went through to the doe, she was also legal. This was the biggest buck I'd ever seen in the wild. I wanted him so badly, and I breathed a "thank you, God" for sending this incredible deer. Like other near-dusk shots, I could see the muzzle flash. All the deer cleared the field in a flurry of white tails. I watched mine run into the thickest of briars, which seems to be the way deer run from me.

Tracking a blood trail is not pleasant in briars, but I knew I'd made a good shot. Funny how that adrenaline helps them run 50 yards, even with a heart shot. When we reached the body, the deer was a one-inch spike buck. I suddenly realized that because of the darkness, the buck had stood parallel <u>behind</u> the big deer (this spike) and not in front. What seemed like an easy-shot and a sure-kill became a great disappointment. I laid in bed and wrestled with the mistake I'd made and the loss of the biggest buck I've ever seen because of it. If I had been more patient or had not been so sure of myself, maybe I'd have that huge rack on my wall. But this is hunting. It's the "chance" of taking the big one, mixed with the chance of seeing nothing, of missing, of falling out of your tree. This is one of hundreds of trips to the woods and more to come. He's still out there. He can count on the fact that I'll be out there, too, when the season comes again.

INSIGHT ONE: High emotion comes in two extremes, good and bad. Part of the challenge of hunting is to continue when things go wrong. Persistence doesn't always pay in hunting and in life, but quitting will guarantee no payoff. Coming so close is exciting in its own way. I remember times of seeing antlers moving through the woods and knowing they were attached to a deer that I could not see or shoot.

Do you remember sports competitions when you were a boy? As time went on and you matured, do you remember how that winning over an easy team was not as exciting as almost beating the championship team? How is that possible? Because "the next time" we were going to do it. If things aren't going that great right now, continue. If you have never succeeded, don't guarantee failure by failing to try again.

INSIGHT TWO: No matter how clearly you "think" you see things, you could have the wrong angle of vision. There could be just enough light to deceive you. I thought the buck crossed in front of what turned out to be a spike. I have stood firm on what I believed to be absolute truth, only to find out that there was one aspect that I had not seen. Until we know everything, we can't be sure that the beliefs, based on what we know, could change with further knowledge. If we want to be correct, we must first acknowledge when we are wrong and change to what is correct. Want to shock your children, your wife? Admit when you're wrong and you will improve your credibility to everyone.

Psalms 42:3: Send forth your light and your truth
let them guide me; let them bring me to your holy mountain,
to the place where you dwell.

CHAPTER TWENTY-EIGHT:
TAKING THE LONG SHOT

It was the first time I'd returned to hunt in Alabama by jet. I had not brought my own gun and would use Dave's old-faithful .308. I knew it was a good gun, and I shot it to be certain it was sighted-in. The pattern of shots were in the bull and within a silver dollar of each other. I allowed a small amount of operator error and felt I was set.

We returned to the Baumhower Plantation where I chose a new and unusual spot to hunt. I was in the bottom by a field, on the edge of a small section of woods and across from a swamp. Nothing moved until noon. Suddenly, from that little section of woods, a long-horned spike buck came running toward me. At fifty yards he stopped and I raised the .380 and shot for the chest. The deer whirled and ran back into the thick little patch of woods. He reappeared about 200 yards out, running with tremendous speed. I pulled up and shot at his chest from broadside. He never flinched but was coming close to a four-foot barbed wire fence. I waited until the peak of his jump, where the deer's upward momentum stops and starts downward, and squeezed. The deer crumpled on the other side of the fence.

It was an amazing shot. I wondered to myself, how can I miss a deer standing at 50 yards and hit at 200 jumping? When I arrived at the deer's body I was really surprised. There was a hole in the frontal chest. I had not missed. There was a hole in the side chest where I had fired as he crossed the field. The third hole was on the backbone, the last shot.

INSIGHT ONE: Never assume that you failed because you don't immediately see the results. Sometimes an effort brings results at a later time. Sometimes we plant a seed now and it sprouts later. We have become a NOW society. Everyone wants what we want right now! The things that take a little longer are often worth waiting for.

INSIGHT TWO: Persistence pays. If I'd not watched for that deer and tried again, the deer would have gone off into the swamp and died. Failure is quitting, not missing. Everyone makes mistakes. At that point we choose whether to go forward or not. Go forward! Try again. Try better. Try a new way. Just don't give up each time it feels like failure.

Even when things look hopeless, hope only dies when we quit. Hope doesn't mean we always hit the jackpot; it is the anticipation that the jackpot is coming.

2 Corinthians 1:10: He has delivered us from such a deadly peril and he will deliver us.
On him we have set our hope that he will continue to deliver us,

CHAPTER TWENTY-NINE:
DAVE, THE PERFECT HUNTER

When I moved to Florida from Alabama, my friend David remained in Tuscaloosa. He continued to hunt regularly, while my Florida friends preferred golf. I mourned and moaned, but made certain to go back each year for four or five days to hunt with David.

It was always a great reunion, then Dave would tell me about the hunts he'd made that year. He got deer with the bow, deer with black powder, and deer with the rifle. All the stories I heard contained no tales of missing. Dave just didn't miss. He was such an excellent hunter that his cover-scent and habits never allowed him to be detected by the deer. He was totally motionless in the woods, and silent.

I was not jealous of Dave. I was glad for him...just sorry for me. I have moved and spooked the deer. They have winded me and snorted. I've been in the wrong position for the shot. The really sad thing is that I believed all the stuff in the previous paragraph. Dave was a great and talented hunter, but he had spooked deer, been scented, and even missed. When we finally had the conversation where he shared some of his boo-boos, I felt much better. You see, we don't tell each other the bad stuff or the mistakes. We like to share the exciting and successful ones. The problem is that the listeners can assume that all of our experiences are positive because that's all they hear from us. That's all we hear from them...except of the closest of friends.

I used to have the same problem with my job. Other pastors would come to conventions and share the way their church grew without any dissension or pastoral errors. I asked God, "Why did you call me to ministry when I'm such a goof-up and you have perfect guys like this?" The answer is simple: they didn't share about their goofs and blunders. That's not why they were paid to come and speak. They came to share their success, and I made the mistake of believing that there was not more to the story than they told. I let myself put "me" down over an artificial idea of the other person's identity. I'd done the same thing with those speakers as I did with Dave...put them on a pedestal that I couldn't reach.

Who is it that you assume always wins? Do you know a guy who succeeds at every venture? Is there a guy at work who just excels every time? Believe me, you need to know the rest of the story. You know all of your experience, good and bad. You don't know theirs. Don't ever believe that there is something wrong with you because you sometimes stumble. That just makes you "normal."

INSIGHT ONE: Be fair to yourself! Don't feel so inferior to those "perfect" people. You don't see their faults and flaws, their secrets and blunders. You can also be blind to your own special features, those gifts and talents God placed in you. Humility is wonderful, but you should know where your talents lie. You should feel good about the things that you do well. Just give God the credit, but don't count yourself out of the equation.

INSIGHT TWO: Heroes are perceived by the beholder! Think about it. The Beatles came to the U.S. like heroes to their adoring fans, while many adults thought they were the anti-Christ. Even Jesus was spit upon by the majority as He came as the hero of God to give His life for all of them. Give yourself a break!

Remember when your kids were little and Dad could do anything? That felt so good. Then the kids became adolescents and you got stupider and stupider (forgive the grammar) in their eyes. Did you change that much, or was it all in the perception of the observer?

So, how do you perceive yourself? You know your motives. Are they pure? You know how much effort you put into each challenge. Was it your best? You are in a position to be very fair to yourself...or very critical of yourself. Be fair, be realistic, and do your best. You know if you've given it all you've got. That's a hero. You can't give what you don't have. God loves you—learn to love yourself.

Jeremiah 29:11: "For I know the plans I have for you," declares the Lord, "plans to prosper you and not to harm you, plans to give you hope and a future."

CHAPTER THIRTY:
MENTORING AN EXPERT

Richard Kiser is an incredible guitarist and hunter (see www.rkisermusic.com), but he'd never shot a wild hog. Living in Florida, I was in a position to make that happen. A friend had the use of a small plot of land out east, toward Myakka City. We got permission and pulled on the camo, the scent kill, took his black powder rifle, and got into position. Rather than climbing the tree stands, we decided to be on the ground in the bushes at one point where the road curved.

We settled down, not talking, and waited...and waited...and waited. There had been a corn feeder in the clearing ahead of us, but it was not functioning. Then that "feeling" came over me that a hunter gets when he's in the woods and an unseen animal is watching him. It's like you feel the animal's presence. This time the animal was not there yet. It was silently approaching and had not seen us. I saw a shadow over Richard's shoulder and motioned with both eyes wide and one finger pointing. Richard's eyes widened, as well, and he smoothly turned with his black powder rifle to find a large black hog coming around the corner. As my friend pulled the trigger, a cloud erupted and the hog was lost in the cloud. When the cloud lifted, the hog was dead on the ground and Richard had another "first" for his hunting experience. Richard is so knowledgeable, yet teachable. I respect a man who is man-enough to learn.

Another man I know had never been deer hunting. He'd read the books and dreamed it, but had not yet experienced the actual hunt. I made arrangements and took my friend out, where he did bag his first deer. From that point on, he became the teacher. He gave me constant advice and instruction in hunting (and there is still much for me to learn), but mostly it felt like disrespect for the fact that I've hunted since I was eleven years old. I hope that I don't seem that way to those I teach. Truthfully, though, I wondered how a man with one hunt under his belt could think himself an authority after simply reading some books. I soon found out that this man considered himself an expert on everything. He just had the kind of personality where he needed to feel "in charge." Those men are usually the ones who are actually the least secure in themselves.

INSIGHT ONE: Richard is a talented hunter with years of experience. Those Virginia hills produce some really nice whitetails, and he has harvested them with rifle, black powder, and bow. Spring turkey season doesn't escape his talents either. I was so thankful to introduce him to a new experience. He has shown me some great things on the guitar, and I got to take him for his first hog. **We learn from each other. It's great to trade-off teaching each other.**

INSIGHT TWO: I think it's wonderful that we can be a student in one situation and still be a teacher in another. Being a student of life shows a lot of wisdom, because we all have much to learn. Even as teachers, we have so much to learn.

I don't enjoy those persons who consider themselves experts in every field. They make me want to put them in their place, which I have a gift for doing (not a Godly gift). That attitude is not worthy of the person that I want to be. Later, when I think about it, I get smarter.

Please realize that many of those with that attitude of being "experts in everything" are actually trying to help. They don't realize how obnoxious and arrogant they can be to those to whom they are trying to impart their vast wisdom. The term "know-it-all" comes to mind, but if we are truly secure in our own masculinity and ability, we can just smile and let it pass. There may even be a few nuggets of wisdom in what they say. So, eat the meat and spit out the bones.

1 Thessalonians 5:11: Therefore encourage one another and build each other up, just as in fact you are doing.

CHAPTER THIRTY ONE:
MY SECOND SON

We loved our first son so much. In fact, we were overwhelmed with the emotion we felt for him. We wanted to protect him and spoil him...and we did. "How great it would be," we thought, "if he had a little brother or sister." Oh, it wouldn't just be for him; we wanted another child.

So, we sat Chris down and had a talk with him at his tender age of four. Would you like a little brother or sister? He said yes and got excited. He got a little toy from Burger King and called it "Amy," his little sister, and carried that toy everywhere he went until his little sister arrived. You can imagine his surprise when Philip arrived. Yes, Philip...a boy.

Let's go back a little ways, though, and I'll share something very personal. We loved our first son so much that we were afraid we wouldn't love the 2nd one the same. I grew up with two younger brothers, and Mom and Dad loved all three of us, but I began to wonder if they loved us all the same.

I soon had an answer. "No, I wouldn't love my two sons the same." They were NOT the same. Chris loved sports and his first word was "ball." It wasn't "Mama" or "Dadda"; it was ball. It sounded like *b-a-a-a-l-l-l*. And we gave him baseballs and footballs and whiffle balls to throw.

Philip loved music. He could pick up an instrument and in no time he was playing it. He finally decided on being a drummer and took lessons. His gift took-off and he could play by notes or by ear. Either way, he was amazing. He wrote arrangements for his drumline in High School and they performed them. He picked up the bass guitar and soon mastered that.

Chris loved music, but sports was his first love. He'd often comment on how easy it was for Philip to play an instrument. Phil was a natural. and Chris had to work hard at it. The great thing was that Chris DID work hard at it, and he's a good guitarist and bass player today, through great effort. I respect than.

I discovered that we didn't love one more than the other. We love both with ultimate love and the pride of parents with great kids. I'd lay down my life for either of them. They're just different than each other.

INSIGHT ONE: There are no two people that we love the same. I love my wife differently than I love my kids. I love my Mom differently than I love my brothers. Love comes in many flavors. Now, my brothers, kids, wife, and Mother have more of my love than others in my life. It's true that love also comes in amounts. But love is great in any amount.

INSIGHT TWO: I show my love for my kids. I hug them, and they are now 30 and 27 years old. I tell them, and they say it back. It's a great thing to look someone in the eye and express what we feel. Oh, I don't tell my hunting buddies, "I love you." I do tell them I appreciate them. I let them know I am thankful to God for them. To tell the truth, when a man is in the hospital, I pray for him and will often say, "I love you, man."

I think love is for doing, not just for feeling. How about you?

John 13:34-35: "A new command I give you: Love one another.(eleventh commandment?)
As I have loved you, so you must love one another.
By this everyone will know that you are my disciples, if you love one another."

CHAPTER THIRTY-TWO:
HUNTING WITH MY YOUNGER SON

I sat quietly in the shooting house with my younger son, Philip. He had slumped over onto my shoulder and fallen asleep, but that was OK. It was his first time hunting. Philip was never interested in hunting. His gifts are in reading, writing, arranging and playing music on the drums, guitar, and bass guitar. It was only a short time as he picked up any instrument, that he could play it. He also is the child who has written books and stories since childhood, first by dictating them to us and later writing by his own hand and illustrating with his own drawings.

So when Chris and I would pack up to go deer hunting, Philip never showed an interest. When the football games were on TV, Philip was not interested. He just kept amazing us with his creativity and musical abilities, even writing musical arrangements for the entire high school band while a student.

One year I received a computer game called "Deer Hunter." You could choose which state to hunt in and where on the topo map to set up your stand. The cover scent was your choice, and you could grunt or be silent. The choice of weapons was your option. Phil started playing the game. That fall, he let me know that he was ready to go hunting.

The light was fading as I sat and watched for both of us. Phil's soft snoring couldn't hold a candle to my own freight train sounds of the night. We would soon need to go back to the cabin. I heard the snap of a small branch breaking and stood up in the stand to look near the base of where we were positioned. That jolted Philip awake, blinking and bleary-eyed. As I raised up, I saw a doe about five yards out from the base of the stand. "There she is," I whispered. I handed Philip the rifle, not knowing if he would actually shoot at the deer or not. As he sighted the deer through the scope, I whispered, "Don't shoot until she turns…" BOOOOMMM! He didn't wait, but he placed the shot well. Soon we were standing over his first deer. The difference between my reaction to my first deer and Philip's reaction was incredible. He had no reaction. It was just a matter of "there's the deer." No emotion was present, no celebration! The doe turned out to be a button buck and would be great eating. The curiosity was satisfied, but Philip just didn't have a real joy of hunting like his Dad. He's not hunting anymore.

Well, guess what? It's OK with me. We're all different. You see, my interests aren't limited to hunting. I love music, as well. I play guitar and am a pretty good vocalist. Philip and I share that interest. I have always been his musical fan, as well as Chris's baseball and football fan. I love my kids for who they are, and they don't have to be exactly like me.

INSIGHT ONE: I admit that having neither son continue to share my excitement and enthusiasm about hunting is a bit of a disappointment. I'm not disappointed in them, however. I love the things that THEY are excited about. I love THEM! **There is no rule that says our kids have to follow in our footsteps in every way.** I just want them to be honest, devoted to God, hard-working, dependable young men, whether they are rocking with a band, playing intramural football, fishing, hunting, writing books, or whatever they choose to do in their leisure time.

INSIGHT TWO: I am not good at everything. I don't have to be. That's why God made other people with other talents. My sons won't have the same talents as I have, and yet they have talents that I can't even approach. The things I'm not talented in do not take away from the fact that I'm very good at other things. Remember that when you watch your son or daughter developing. Cheer them on the good stuff and encourage them in their development of areas that need help.

INSIGHT THREE: Finding what you don't like to do is also success. We could waste valuable time trying to be a pro football player when we're really more talented as an administrator for a large corporation. I often thought of the young ladies I dated and decided were not "the one." That was success! Marrying the wrong one would be failure. The same is true of our talents, hobbies, and professions. We need to find the one that brings us pleasure, joy, and fulfillment, and we all won't like the same ones. When your child determines not to be the doctor you'd always dreamed of, rejoice in the choice he or she makes.

> *1 Corinthians 12:4: There are different kinds of gifts, but the same Spirit.*
> *5 There are different kinds of service, but the same Lord.*
> *6 There are different kinds of working, but the same God works all of them in all men.*

CHAPTER THIRTY THREE:
MAMA'S BOY
(DON'T YOU MESS WITH MY MAMA.)

As a child, if you want something fixed, you take it to Dad. Dad can fix anything. On the other hand, if you get hurt, scrape your knee, or bang your head, you go to Mom. She's the one who can make it all better, who comforts her little child and kisses the wound.

I remember lying in my bed upstairs in our house on Rebecca Street. All was peaceful, and I was never afraid up there with my two younger brothers because Mom and Dad were downstairs and any monsters would have to get through them to get to the stairs and come to our room. The peacefulness that night was not there. I strained to hear the words, but couldn't. I could hear the loud voices, though. They were not happy. Mom and Dad were having problems again. In a while I heard the door slam, and I knew that Dad had left the building. I could hear sobs down the stairs. I wasn't allowed to get out of bed, but I did it anyway. Mom was crying.

She was sitting on the bottom step with her head in her hands, quietly weeping. I slipped down the stairs and put my arms around her, saying, "Mom, it will be alright." I just held her while she cried.

My parents divorced, and I had a single mother. I was now the man of the house, and everyone told me so. So I comforted Mom when she cried, I washed dishes, and swept the floors to have a clean house before she got home from work. I even learned to cook and would have dinner on the table when she got home from working at Sears. I walked my younger brothers to school and picked them up afterwards at 11 years old.

So you could say I was a Mama's boy and it won't phase me. I would think in terms of the man of the house, but I loved my Mom and that was it. You could say what you want about me, but don't you talk bad about my mama. She worked and gave us affection, and sacrificed. She was always there. She rubbed our backs when we were throwing up in the toilet. She was a nurse, a mom, a cook, a provider.

Oh, I loved my Dad. I got to see him every other weekend, stay in a motel, and eat all our meals at restaurants. He loved us in his own way. He was not affectionate until he later became a grandpa, but he became a terrific grandpa and a more loving dad.

I'm very much older now, but I'm still my Mama's boy. I'd still fight for her, whatever that now means. I want to provide for her. I want her to know that she is still needed and wanted in my life. I want her to know how grateful I am that she gave herself so sacrificially for many years. Was she perfect? No. Was she magnificent? Yes.

INSIGHT ONE: I learned how to be a parent by copying the good and avoiding the shortcomings in my folks. There was so much more good than bad. Am I or was I ever a perfect parent? No, but my children can also copy my good and avoid my shortcomings. Nobody knows the good and the shortcomings like they do. By the way, I am still learning to be a parent. It's tough, because my kids keep changing and maturing, and the learning curve never stops.

INSIGHT TWO: Love is not just a feeling. Feelings are side effects, but love is commitment. Love is sacrifice of self for the other. I learned most of that from my Mom.

Mark 10:19: You know the commandments: 'You shall not murder, you shall not commit adultery,
you shall not steal, you shall not give false testimony, you shall not defraud,
honor your father and mother.'"

CHAPTER THIRTY-FOUR:
SCOUTING FOR A LIFE PARTNER— THE ULTIMATE HUNT

I've been lucky in choosing my hunting spots. When I choose them, I consider the traffic pattern of the deer, the direction of the wind, scouting determinations, and other factors. I don't just randomly go out and hunt. As a result, I've had a lot of luck.

I waited until age 24 to choose a wife. It's not that I was ready then, but I was ready to be ready. My dating had been varied and careless, but finally something clicked in my mind. The others had been great girls, but this girl was different than the others. I saw features in this person that I truly enjoyed more. My face smiled, my heart smiled, and I just enjoyed her. I moved more slowly this time. I watched the "signs" and found that the chances of success were terrific.

Why, then, was I so careless about dating? Fact is, we can fall in love with the wrong one if we don't shop where we intend to buy. I mean, if I want to buy a new Jeep, I don't go to the Hyundai dealership. So, if I realize that my dating may lead to the discovery of the woman I would marry, I should date the kind of girl I think I want for myself, for the mother of my children, and for the rest of my life. Let's have some fun with this...

I dated a lot. I mean a whole lot. Though I am now overweight and lukewarm at best, I used to be "hot." No, really. So I dated some real "babes" out there. They looked so good, but the wonder is that many of them didn't look so good when I got to know them. When we see character flaws, it brings out all the flaws, and I certainly have my own. I began to discover that I really wanted a friend with whom I was very attracted. I wanted someone who would love and nurture my children. I wanted a woman who treated her family well and was not selfish, because I was more and more ready to sacrifice for the happiness of a life partner.

I always chuckled at my friends who carefully chose what car to buy, but carelessly and randomly dated whomever would "make out" on a date or who dressed so great. Tell me guys, if you marry a girl for the way she dresses, who pays for the dresses for the rest of her life? If she's all over you in the backseat of your car, whose backseat was she in last week? Who did you have in your backseat last week?

After years of dating, I found a girl I enjoyed joking and spending time with. I'd often kissed a girl before the first date, just to make sure she was a good kisser. How dumb! I spent five weeks of campus time with the latest girl, studying, playing, walking, talking, laughing, eating...and never even tried to kiss her. Finally, I broke the ice with a little kiss and we both smiled. Within a year, we were married—best friends, husband and wife, lovers, partners. It was the best choice I ever made. I scouted her, watched her, and what I saw was awesome. Some thirty years later, we're still best friends, lovers, husband and wife, parents, co-workers in the church, roommates, and someday we'll be grandparents. I just hope my sons find someone as great as I did.

You young hunters and fishermen, don't let marriage just happen to you. CHOOSE your life partner. Your bodies will change and age, but the "person" of your choice is so important. Shop where you intend to buy, guys. Find someone with your same values and faith. Find someone you love to sacrifice for and who appreciates that about you. Find a great mom for your kids, someone you'd really enjoy spending the rest of your life with as your best friend.

INSIGHT ONE: Life is not what happens to you as you move toward death. It comes one day at a time. Much of what we go through is the result of choices we made earlier, and the choices of those closest to us. One of the most important choices you will ever make is the choice of your partner for life.

INSIGHT TWO: Happiness is often learning to want what you've got, rather than getting what you want. Yes, you read this statement in an earlier chapter, but read it again. Remember that the woman you choose is also making a choice. If she chooses you, she is choosing you over all the other men in the world. Cool, huh? Been married 10 or 20 years? Good for you. Are you still trying to make the relationship better? Are you aware of what you have? Many guys take it all for granted and then look back to realize how great that woman was. Others end up with the "other woman," who doesn't really look so good as a permanent partner. Don't throw a treasure away for a pleasure.

Proverbs 18:22: He who finds a wife finds what is good and receives favor from the Lord.

CHAPTER THIRTY-FIVE:
TRUE FRIENDS? WHEN FRIENDS DON'T WANT YOU ANYMORE.

One of my hunting friends began as a stranger. He had gone through a terrible life crisis that involved a death. I met him and stood with him through that time, listening to him, spending time with him, and praying with him. Those were the years when I had few places to hunt. When I finally got an opportunity, I invited him to go with me and we took his first hunting trip together, resulting in his first doe. Later, when I had another opportunity, I invited him again and he shot his first buck.

In years to come, he found some places to hunt when I had none. He hunted, but I was not invited. Being a better friend to my friends than they are to me was nothing new in my life. I can't change them, but I can do what I feel is right. I have no control over them, but I can control the kind of friend that I am. Think of it this way: men who are great friends to others are rare, unique, and special. We humans are selfish in nature, and those who aren't are unusual and wonderful. When your friends don't return the same concern and kindness, they just aren't as gifted as you are.

The man and I worshiped together for some time, and I watched the wonder of his healing. I have always loved "giving" to my friends. It gives me joy to make a difference in their lives. In fact, I have a difficulty avoiding becoming their caretaker, rather than simply a caregiver.

After giving concern, time, and caring to this man for many years, he suddenly rejected my friendship. That's hard for me to understand, but I see it happening in the lives of others often. Someone you have grown with and shared with is suddenly ready to cast you off and out of their life. We will likely never hunt again. I grieved, but I have doubts about whether he did.

INSIGHT ONE: People can turn on you. Sometimes they'll be people you never would have suspected, but they suddenly desire to hurt you. Very few of them were truly friends to begin with. Some are just misled. Some are justified. Some people are our friends and others are pretty-much consumers. They'll consume whatever we're willing to give and share, then when we're dry or need help, they're gone.

If you've had the experience and now question your worth, let me point out that Jesus came and was rejected by most people. Even Peter denied him three times. Others ran away when Jesus was faced with danger in the Garden of Gethsemane.

The guy in my illustration was a consumer. I can't think of one thing he ever did for me, but I never noticed that before because I was committed to the friendship. Maybe he thought it was enough to simply accept me. My understanding was different from his. I loved sacrificing to give him good things. Only after his rejection did I realize that I had only lost a dependant and not a friend...but I still grieved his loss because my friendship was not conditional.

Psalm 41:9: Even my close friend, whom I trusted, he who shared my bread, has lifted up his heel against me.

INSIGHT TWO: Life goes on, even after a friend turns on you. Oh, it hurts, but you can't take a time-out and forget all your other friends and life projects. Live on, even as you grieve. Don't be afraid to trust again. **Don't lose friendships to come by living in the pain of friendships past.**

INSIGHT THREE: We only have the opportunity to truly invest long term in the lives of a few people. We can't handle too many dependants. Our resources are limited. It's wise to plant our seeds in the fields where our seed will grow. **Some of us need to change our circle of associates and find someone who is a friend.**

Friends want the best for us. They're not looking for someone to keep them company as they fail. Misery loves company, but success does, too. If you're not bringing your friends UP, then they are dragging you down. Move on if you are being dragged down.

Proverbs 17:17: A friend loves at all times, and a brother is born for adversity.

Jesus spent a lot of time with drunks and sinners. Religious leaders criticized Him for that, but they were wrong. He wasn't sinking with them. He was there to bring them UP. He was a friend to people who weren't committed to Him, but He was their source of rescue. There are some folks you can rescue and others who will bring you low. There are some friends who want to give to you and others who want to simply use you up and throw you away. Choose your friends and companions wisely. Invest well.

True Friends? When Friends Don't Want You Anymore.

*Proverbs 18:24: A man of many companions may come to ruin, but there is a **friend** who sticks closer than a brother.*

CHAPTER THIRTY-SIX:
QUICKSAND

It was a trout fishing trip near Clarion, Pennsylvania, and a beautiful day. I took my friend, Chris, with us to Cather's Run that day, and we were all outfitted with hip waders for the event. The stream had only one direction and we entered from the end of it, where it emptied into the Clarion River. No one would get lost, because we simply needed to follow the stream.

As we approached an inlet, I had a choice of crossing in the shallow water or walking around the inlet on the land. I chose the shallow water; I mean, what are hip waders for? Chris chose to go around. I would have been to the other side very quickly, but the mud beneath the shallow water began to suck at the waders and pull me under. I had made it most of the way and had only a few feet to go, but I could not lift my feet. They were stuck in that mud and I was still sinking. Chris had made it to the other side and was standing there in shock as I sunk lower.

I was scared, yelling to Chris, "Pull me out!" He stood there staring, not knowing what to do. The water was now pouring into my boots as I'd sunk past the tops of them. In desperation, I lunged toward Chris and grabbed his arm. "Chris, pull me out or I'm pulling you in." He pulled me out!

INSIGHT ONE: Desperation can push us into doing things we wouldn't normally do. While love can lead us to sacrifice for our friends, desperation can cause us to sacrifice our friends for ourselves. My friend would not normally leave me there to sink, but sometimes fear and shock can cause our friends to let us down because they don't know how to react. Chris and I went on being friends after that experience, although I'm not certain where he might be today! I'm just glad I'm still here.

INSIGHT TWO: When our friends are in trouble, there are times to get in there and pull them out. Truth is, however, sometimes they don't see that they are sinking and won't allow you to pull them out. They may even reject you. Drugs, affairs, alcohol, and workaholicism are some things that may suck us in without our realizing it. When your realize you are sinking, don't be afraid to call for help. You'd help if your friend was sinking. When your friend rejects you, don't go too far away. He may wake up from his anger or stupor and realize his need soon.

*Psalm 124:7: We have escaped like a bird out of the fowler's snare; the snare has been broken,
and we have escaped. 8 Our help is in the name of the Lord, the Maker of heaven and earth.*

CHAPTER THIRTY-SEVEN:
THE DARKEST FOURTH OF JULY

There were no big fireworks on the fourth of July at our cabin in the woods when I was growing up. We didn't care! It was just so great being in the woods. The extent of our celebration was usually a box of sparklers, which my two brothers and I would run around the yard holding in our hands. We didn't need a party, because we were a party already.

No one drank alcohol at our cabin. We didn't need to do that in order to have fun. Life had its own highs. There was often a "high" in just being together. On this particular 4th of July, my step dad was in an unusually good mood. He grabbed his shotgun, loaded a shell and jumped onto the front porch to fire into the air. There was no planning involved. That became obvious when his shot blew all the electrical wires off the cabin and all the lights went out. That would also mean no cooking, since the range was electric, and no air conditioning for the rest of the weekend.

His unusually good mood instantly changed to his usually stoic one, and we all groaned silently. This meant a lousy weekend was underway, but we began to play a game. Where are the candles? Can we cook over the fireplace? Let's open the windows and sleep in the woods air tonight. We'd brought the party right back into the weekend and the rest of the weekend went well.

The next morning my step dad (who was very handy around the house) fixed the wires and we shared our amazement at how many things he could do. It was true, and also improved his mood again. That night for supper, however, we still used the candles and turned out the lights.

INSIGHT ONE: When things are going well, don't let one incident ruin it all. Choose to see the best, rather than sinking into the depths of depression. Our party doesn't have to end because someone blew the lights out.

INSIGHT TWO: Building people up is always a good idea. We built my step dad up because it made him easier to live with. Truthfully, however, it also made his life better for that time. It's amazing that we have the power to either build or smash people. Mostly, I see a lot of smashing going on out there. We can choose to use the power of our mouth either way. If we truly have a choice, what will we choose?

Colossians 4:6: Let your conversation be always full of grace, seasoned with salt, so that you may know how to answer everyone.

Ephesians 4:29: Do not let any unwholesome talk come out of your mouths, but only what is helpful for building others up according to their needs, that it may benefit those who listen.

CHAPTER THIRTY-EIGHT:
TALKIN' TURKEY

I was sitting at the base of a tree, wearing camouflage, with leafy branches surrounding me. The tree broke my silhouette and the leaves did the same. Gun ready, I pulled the cedar box turkey call from my pocket and began to yelp. I don't have a lot of experience with calling, but I was really excited to get a big gobble from just over the hill. I didn't want to call too much, so I figured it was better to hold back and not over-call. Men love the chase, right? So why not male turkeys? It seemed to work, because each time I did yelp two or three times, the gobbler answered, but he didn't come in. He was so loud that I knew he wasn't far, but he wouldn't move. I didn't move either. I've been warned again and again that the turkey's vision is incredible. So I sat camouflaged, against a big tree and behind leafy brush, motionless.

After about two hours of yelp-gobble, yelp-gobble, I was getting frustrated with this gobbler. In my mind I was lecturing the bearded-one, "If you're too shy, the girl will move on, dude!" But I sat motionless and continued to yelp. He kept answering. Finally, I couldn't stand it any longer. I crawled to the edge of the next hollow on my belly, an inch at a time and peered over a log that was lying across the edge.

He was a big one with a long beard, maybe 250 pounds, wearing camo, sitting against a tree. I'm not sure where he learned to gobble, but he was good at it and did it with an in-the-mouth caller. He never knew I was there as I backed away, stood and made my way to the car. I thought about what might have happened if that other hunter had inched his way up the hill to peer over to my side. I can hear him thinking, "He's a big one, no beard, but maybe 250 pounds..."

By the way, I've shot high numbers of deer, maybe thirty wild hogs, lots of rabbits and pheasant, but I've never scored a turkey. I've hunted the mountain-to-mountain fall rifle season in Pennsylvania and the spring gobbler season in Florida and Alabama, but no turkey. Will I surrender? Will I quit the pursuit of that elusive bird? No! The challenge just keeps getting greater. One day maybe you'll read about it in one of my stories.

INSIGHT ONE: Even when we don't accomplish our goal, the process can be a lot of fun! I thought I was pitting my limited calling skills against a wily bird, when I was actually just yelping in conversation with another knuckle-headed hunter. I had fun all morning, however, just talkin' turkey and thinking I was close to a trophy.

Life can be like that. We need to make the journey part of the adventure...not just the arrival. Even in tasks where I didn't succeed, there was often a source of pride just giving my best (and occasionally a lot of embarrassment) .

If there were not the possibility of failure, there would be no thrill in success. Those times when I hunted or fished and came home empty-handed made the next trip more challenging and the next trophy more fulfilling. If you're not succeeding, maybe the next time will bring the success.

INSIGHT TWO: Blending-in doesn't assure success. Check the other parts of your methods. My camo was excellent, and I was in a good position against that tree. Still no turkey! Being in the right place at the right time was not the case that day.

A lot of life's success looks like luck. Sometimes **preparation** is the key. The right **timing** is vital. The **right place** is essential. That's four: luck, preparation, timing, and placement. No one thing will assure success, but all four can increase the probability of success. A lot of people just let life happen to them. They make no provision, no preparation. They don't scout the potential or check the time. I like to have more going for me than luck.

If you're not having success at anything in your life, check your plan and methods. Have you prepared? Is the timing right? Don't give up just because luck hasn't hit. One more thing—is the goal worthwhile? Maybe it's time to put the preparation and time into something better. Oh, let me add a number 5: design. Y'see, I believe God loves to bless His kids (that's us) and has a plan laid out for us in life, so I ask Him to give me some wisdom in my direction so that I don't miss any of those blessings.

Luke 12:22: Then Jesus said to his disciples:"Therefore I tell you, do not worry about your life, what you will eat; or about your body, what you will wear. 23 Life is more than food, and the body more than clothes. 24 Consider the ravens: They do not sow or reap, they have no storeroom or barn; yet God feeds them. And how much more valuable you are than birds!"

POSTLUDE:
WHO AM I?

My Concept of God

I'm not a religious guy, but I am totally amazed by Jesus. I have never worshiped the church, but I do worship the One who founded it. God never meant those churches to be rest homes or private clubs for religious people, even though many become that. He meant for us to BE the church and go out, impact lives, encourage others, enjoy His creations, share the good stuff we learn, and make life better for our family and others.

Am I in a church? Yep! Because I know the Big Guy who started it, I am a part of a church and love it.

We outdoorsmen really understand God's beautiful creation because we see that His beautiful creation proves that there is a Creator. Picture your hunting and fishing area and you'll likely smile. I'm so glad He created all that beauty.

It's just natural to me to share the stories that make me smile. I think God must really laugh out loud at our antics sometimes. He's not up there with a giant flyswatter, looking for us to mess up so that he can swoooosh and swat us. He loves us, and He's looking for people who need His blessing. He's working to keep us out of the many "hells" we bring upon ourselves. The Bible says He doesn't want any to perish.

My Attention Deficit Disorder Mind

I'm ADD (attention deficit disorder) My mind never stops. I think and process all day and dream all night. I get out of bed in the middle of the night to write new thoughts down before I forget. My car is littered with napkins and pieces of paper with notes I pull over and make. I live ten hunts in my imagination and dreams before I ever go on a real one. My brain never rests, but I don't want a less active mind. I'll keep this active one. Every day is an adventure of pursuing, planning, discovering, creating, recognizing blessing, imagining, stumbling, getting up again, and overcoming hardships.

My Highly Developed Sense of Hearing

As I get older, I find that my hearing and sight aren't what they used to be, but may still be better than average in the woods. Sorting all the noises of squirrels, running streams, and distant traffic from the crack of a twig disturbed by a big buck is still possible. I'm really good at hearing my wife call me to supper. I can barely hear her at all when she calls me to take the garbage to the curb. Sound familiar?

My location as I write?

I'm sitting here in a cabin in the gorgeous woods of Roan Mountain, Tennessee. The trees and undergrowth are so thick that there is no view of anything distant. Just green! I hear Roaring Creek in the hollow, but I can't see it. It's like the many times I feel God sharing with me, leading and inspiring me, so powerful but not visible. A big deck porch spans the front of this cabin with one double rocker and two individual rocking chairs. This is not "roughing it." There is hot water, a full bathroom, kitchen, a queen-sized bed and this is luxury. To add to that luxury, I have my wife with me, doing her own thing. We are isolated with lots of relaxation and thinking time. The cellphone seldom rings because service is poor. I've shot my bow and arrow each day whenever I feel like it. This is luxury.

FAREWELL FOR NOW! Thanks for sharing some of these experiences with me. There is a thing called vicarious learning, where we learn the lesson from seeing another guy's experience. It's a good and bad deal: you get to learn the lesson without experiencing the pain... or the joy.

I hope you learned some of the things I've learned...and maybe a few I have yet to learn. I hope you realize that all men wrestle with life, and occasionally we win the wrestling match. Either way, life is an adventure worth living. The ways we perceive it and the goals we set, along with the decisions we make about how we approach and love people, make it a lot better. Have an adventure today...and tomorrow... and the next day...

God bless you.
Bro

CPSIA information can be obtained
at www.ICGtesting.com
Printed in the USA
FSHW010708290120
66547FS